SALIENT SALES & TRAINING

growing businesses by developing sales

THE PERSUASIVE POWER OF ETHICAL SELLING

The skills and expertise to sell effectively in any market

Presented by Andrew Entwistle B.Sc., F.I.S.M.

Salient Sales & Training......talk with experience

Andrew Entwistle BSc, FInstSMM
& associates 01793 843118
Mob 07941 041364
andyentwistle@salientsales.co.uk
www.salientsales.co.uk

Published by Andrew Entwistle, MD of Salient Sales & Training

The moral rights of the author have been asserted.

A catalogue record of this book is available from the British Library.
ISBN No: 978-1-9161728-0-7

Proofing and editing: Angela Clarence
Cover design: Adam Vine of Lounge Design
Printed by Glyn Miller of Chivers Design and Print
Page layout by David Rolls of White Star Design

ACKNOWLEDGEMENTS

I could name many more, but would like to note the following
Thanks:
to the many bosses, colleagues and friends gained throughout an eventful career in selling, to name but a few: Ken Turrell, Richard Ayres, Chris Harris, Vic Slawinski, John Lavery, John Lane, Alan Longland, Steve Edwards....
to the many customers and friends (sometimes they were both), in particular: Andy Hudson, George Seward, Andy Poulton, Gary Curzon, David Joel, Stuart Allinson, Tony Wragg, Andy Case, Michael Trigg, Anthony Stears, Giles Lloyd.......
And, my family for their endless love and support; particularly for my wife Sarah who copes wonderfully with my very occasional eccentricities!

The list is potentially huge, so my apologies to anyone who feels left out.

TESTIMONIALS

Highly professional and fulfilling today's demand; really well explained.
– Ajay Singh, Sales Manager, Samsung LEDs GmbH

Excellent and informative
– Colleen Roberts, Technical Sales Manager, GSF Slides

Andy is insightful and professional. He offers great tips and advice for moving businesses forward.
– Reshma Field, Style Consultant and owner of Ishbel's Wardrobe.

I strongly recommend Salient. Andy explains in an easy to understand manner. Plenty to implement.
– Dominic Elves, MD of Pure Boilers

The course will have a positive impact on our company
- Simon Parkinson; Director of PSR Ltd Halifax (Course delivered to 10 delegates)

The course was very good particularly in simplifying the concepts.
- Les Gaskell; Technical Director

An excellent week, time well spent.
- Colin Robinson: Sales Office Manager

Working with Salient provided a great opportunity to see things objectively and with different perspectives. This was very valuable.
– Simon Kent, Director, Sollertis

I would recommend Andy to anyone who needs some sales advice or would like to grow their business to the next stage. I would encourage 'coaching sceptics' to see Andy and experience true value!
– Ben Franks, CEO Novel Wines

I found the course very informative and it gave me lots of ideas.
– Jan Lewis, Sales Coordinator, Ortlinghaus UK Ltd.

FOREWORD

By Giles Lloyd, Director of Sales & Marketing at Wilson Electric (Battersea) Ltd.

Do people really buy from people?

At the age of 22, I fell into procurement via a recruitment agency – over the next 8 years, I worked my way through three roles, progressing, studying and becoming qualified, but still finding myself looking for a sense of fulfilment. One afternoon as I'm sat in the office I began talking with the national sales manager, we had always got on well however the conversation usually only went as far as asking me to run statistical reports on product lines or increase safety stocks. His frustration in attempting to find the right candidate for a vacant area sales manager role at the company was evident, having just walked another unsuccessful candidate out the door – the role had been open for a couple of months. I jokingly said to him, "I'll have a go!", fast forward 3 years and I am Director of Sales and Marketing at one of the most well-established mechanical engineering companies in London and the UK.

My name is Giles Lloyd. During my career in procurement I had become used to the typical 'pushy salesperson', you know the one – they'll push a sale at any cost, often excessively pressuring you to buy promising the world whilst wrapping you up in jargon. Many salespeople had walked through the door with this tact and walked right back out without a sale. It's a complete turn-off. The exact opposite of the salesperson that I wanted to become.

Luckily for me, within a few weeks of venturing into sales, my manager had enrolled my peers and I onto a Technical Sales Training & Coaching course run by Andy Entwistle. I'd never met Andy prior to his training, but I can honestly say that my rapid ascension within 'sales' and my chosen industry is due in no small part to the knowledge and training imparted on me by Andy and his belief in the persuasive power of ethical selling. Within a three-and-a-half-year period I had transformed the sales in the area I was responsible for (the south-east of the UK)- the turnover had doubled and loyal customers that were once prospects I'd identified for business were giving me regular repeat business with ease.

Ethical selling is the only way forward. Honesty, integrity and simplicity. Business is built on relationships.

It's imperative for me to make sure that the buyer is sold on me before they are sold on the product that I am selling – this is key. In fact, as long as I am sold and passionate about the product I am selling, then the prospect will be too. This was something that was very clear about Andy from the moment I met him – his passion for ethical selling was evident, infectious and easy to follow.

This book contains extremely powerful information which will revolutionise the way that you approach and see sales. Never underestimate the importance of marketing to sales (marketing the product and marketing yourself!), which when executed correctly makes your job a lot easier bringing business to you negating the need for prospecting and the dreaded 'cold call' (or are they hot contacts? – see Chapter 5 for clarification).

How about prospecting and finding new business? Who is the M.A.N.? Could your existing customers work for you and bring you new business? You bet they can! Considering the points that I have discussed with you – can we closing the deal? Learn 'The Ultimate Close' to ensure that you get the desired result from the negotiation that is the best for you, and your customer.

Everything that I learnt from Andy's 'Salient Sales & Training' is contained within these pages and will provide you with the complete repertoire of tools needed to become the very salesperson that I wanted to be – one of respect that did exactly what I said I would do for my customer, reliable and adaptable to their needs to make my offering the only viable solution.

By adopting the techniques laid out in this book I am sure that you will create a strong recipe for success that is repeatable, time and time again. The information is universally applicable whether you are an experienced salesperson, or are new to it as I was the first time I learnt the persuasive power of ethical selling.

To answer the question of 'Do people really buy from people?' – Yes, absolutely, people like me buy from people like you.

Giles Lloyd, Director of Sales & Marketing at Wilson Electric (Battersea) Ltd.

MY STORY

I started my career as a qualified physicist. I loved everything to do with physics and science in general. Finally achieving a degree in the subject, I looked around for suitable occupations. Pure or even applied physics jobs were few and far between, so I did what most physicists did in the early 80s and became an electronics engineer.

The 'fun' of designing and building circuits soon wore off. Luckily at this point, the company offered to move me to 'Applications Engineering'. This was great as I was to advise and assist the sales team in all technical aspects of the specialist circuits they were selling. In those days, it was common for an engineer who had any social and conversational skills to be asked to become a Sales Engineer. After a couple of job moves it finally happened to me. My response? Well, they offered me a car. Early 20s, an 'executive' car; no contest.

I spent the next 20 years in the field, first as a sales engineer, then as a sales manager and finally director. In 2004, situations conspired to make me re-evaluate my life and, to cut a long story short, I 'jacked-it-in'. I lost a lot of money, recovered my life, reduced the blood pressure, and started smiling again. I promoted myself as Freelance Technical Sales and for three years I was able to fully develop my sales processes, skills and techniques. Finally, I took the plunge and formed Salient Sales & Training: a company focused on helping people and businesses to find more customers and win more sales.

When I started Salient back in 2007, I had 20 years of selling and sales management experience. I had devised my own sales process and I had a multitude of thoughts and ideas; some complete but many still in various stages of development. Like most business leaders I met, I looked at what was available in the market, what other sales systems were out there. Apparently, it was common practice when you started out to 'borrow and adapt' other people's ideas, structures and even tag lines and tips.

Everywhere I looked, 'sales experts' were pushing and promoting their 'fool-proof, successful, panaceas for sales growth'. Many were contradictory; most were highly complex, and I remember one even encouraged 'threatening' as a negotiation technique!

There were ***some*** good ideas out there, but I decided to start from scratch and define what I had already proved to be successful.

I decided to take things back to their simplest and most easily understood forms and to develop a flexible approach to my selling skills and techniques; the ones I had been using productively over many years but had never written down.

It took time, but I have now been presenting, training, coaching and mentoring this approach for nearly ten years. In that time, it has been tweaked, honed, improved and perfected. The contents of this book comprise the most essential parts for your consideration and for you to use as you see fit.

Over that twenty years in sales I was, for the most part, selling for someone else in the corporate world. Clashes were inevitable from time to time. (Some juicy details later). Mainly, these happened because I had my ideas of how sales and selling should be conducted, but I was working for people whose opinions were based around the philosophy that 'the end justifies the means'; the end was to 'exceed target' and the means involved various practices- many not ethical!

I came across methods involving everything from slight exaggeration of the product, to out and out lies, and even threats to sales personnel and customers. So, I did it my way, which, on more than one occasion resulted in threats of job loss. Yet 9 times out of 10 my way was proven to be right- and the tenth was simply impossible to prove!

My way of thinking was simple:

- People buy from people they like
- Buyers are not stupid
- Treat buyers well and they will buy more
- Treat buyers badly and they will go elsewhere
- If buyers lack loyalty, it puts the sales personnel under pressure to find more and more new customers and
- Sales personnel under pressure pass the pressure on to the customer...and so the negative cycle continues

When an MD said to a former colleague 'If you don't win the business don't bother coming back' so he did anything and everything to win that business, but did he win the business? I'll tell you later!

The fact is, I had a better ethos, a better way of selling- based on building relationships that resulted in trust and loyalty- so my customers kept coming back!

When I had had enough of the end justifies the means business culture and at a time which coincided with family health issues, I finally left the corporate world. I became a freelance sales resource which allowed me to prove, hone and develop the Salient Sales Process.

By December 2007 the process was ready, and I formed ***'Salient Sales and Training'*** as the company set to ***change the world...one business at a time!*** Since then I have trained or coached people from over 100 companies and can say with some conviction, that I have made a positive difference in every case. My job satisfaction is excellent, and I am hugely grateful to all my clients, past and present. Thank you.

THE SALIENT SALES HANDBOOK

CONTENTS

CHAPTER 1

THE PERSUASIVE POWER OF ETHICAL SELLING

The Book of the System of the Process of the Magic of Business Development (formerly known as sales).

How to Sell More, More Effectively and More Often - with a system that can apply to any business

What makes this one different?

- ***Ethical*** *- no pressure!*
- ***Jargon-free*** *- understandable*
- ***Proven*** *- over 20 years in the field*
- ***Simple*** *- a common sense approach*
- ***Highly effective*** *- high conversions achieved*
- ***Fully adaptable*** *- to your business and approach*
- ***Repeatable*** *- instils high loyalty and repeat business*

And NOT manipulative of customers, pressuring, unnecessarily complex, or inflexible!

Being **simple** and **adaptable**, this system makes it easier to make a sale, which also makes the process **motivational**, providing great job-satisfaction. Being **ethical** helps you to sleep at night. And being **proven** and **repeatable** makes this book a fantastic return on your investment!

WHERE DID IT COME FROM?

It may be a cliché, but I *love* helping people. The greatest job satisfaction for me is seeing someone take an idea that was born and developed in a Salient course or session and use it to make a significant positive difference to them and their business. And it is rare that a client leaves such a session with only one such idea. Many will take the whole system and apply it to great positive effect. I feel lucky to be in a position where I can now make this happen on a frequent basis.

This book will give you insight into the Salient Sales System. You will find it simple, full of common sense and completely adaptable to any business. The skills, techniques and tips described and provided within the book have all been tried and tested on numerous occasions.

Some of these will work very effectively for you, so choose the ones that fit your beliefs, your ethos and your business, and have a go. Each one used well will make a positive difference. Use a few of them and you will make a big difference to your success. Use them all, and your sales will start to see a significant improvement.

Any individual from any size and type of market, in any size of business, from global to entrepreneur, will benefit from this book. I have a specialisation in Technical Sales Training – selling into technical markets. While this book does not cover the extra layers of knowledge needed for technical sales, it includes many general sales skills, strategies and techniques that will benefit all.

I finished this book a while ago. Then the General Data Protection Regulation and the Privacy and Electronic Communications Regulation came into effect. Luckily only a few small adjustments were needed (as you would expect from an ethical sales process!) The requirements relate to methods of contacting and to the storage of customer data. Key details relevant to sales and marketing are covered in this book.

The majority of chapters are set out in the same order as the modules which form the courses I present, that make up the Salient Sales System. Each module takes anything from a couple of hours to a couple of days to cover, depending on the client's needs.

While the chapters cannot cover every aspect of the course modules,
I have picked the 'best bits' which are easiest to grasp and apply.
(For help in the application of these skills to your business, please do get in touch.)

The book ends with 'Securing or Closing the Deal', however, we all know this is not, and should not be the end of it. It is essential to have strategies, skills and techniques for customer or client development. After the sale, if you do not look after and continue developing your relationship, someone else will step in and undo all the good work you have done to win that business. Customer Development will be the large and essential subject of the book which will follow this or will become its first major revision. I will let you know when it is ready!

Selling to people is often regarded as confrontational whereas the Salient ethos and the basis of what I teach is:

- To build positive relationships and
- To help people buy wisely to fulfil their need

After more than 20 years in the field I am happy to confirm that this approach will help you to form the most stable and loyal customer base from which to grow your business.

There is one particular word choice I wish to clarify. I sometimes refer to 'controlling the sales process'. I generally add the words 'or lead' to this. Controlling can imply restriction of the buyers' options in a potentially manipulative way. Likewise, the idea to 'lead' the sales process may be too passive for some. As an ethical sales handbook, I can only suggest that ***you*** choose how much you should control and how much you should lead!

In training and coaching it is all very well showing people how it can be done more successfully and enjoying those wonderful 'eureka' or light-bulb moments, but too often this a temporary result. Human nature intervenes and, within a few months old habits are back, and the benefits dilute to nothing. For this reason, I also encourage delegates to book refresher courses to re-focus and ensure new initiatives are repeated enough to become embedded in their routine.

The book has also been written in such a way as to allow you to return easily to the various sections and refresh your memory of the ideas, tips and techniques. Read it and read it again. If you like the ideas, try them, adapt and adopt them. If they work, embed them and enjoy them. If they don't, move on and try the next tip or technique.

If any of the points and ideas give you cause for concern, or help you to celebrate success, please feel free to offer feedback as I would be very pleased to offer help in the former and join in the latter!

My first principal in business is to give value. What better way of giving value than to encourage you to read the book again and again and learn more each time! My other business principles are integrity, professionalism and good humour. I hope you find all of these in equal measure within the pages of this book. Enjoy....

CHAPTER 2

MARKETING FOR SALES

This is a sales handbook. However, it also focuses on the bigger picture often called 'Business Growth'. ***When growing a business, salespeople need to work closely with and alongside the marketing discipline.*** In many larger companies, sales and marketing are separated as two individual disciplines and departments. Too often, the communication between these departments is lacking and the marketing material does not always match the claims of the sales personnel...and vice versa!

Sales and marketing should work together because they are defined thus:

MARKETING: *raising your profile in the market and attracting new customers*

SALES: *presenting, negotiating, and closing the deal with new 'prospects' then managing & developing them into regular 'clients'*

Without good marketing, sales activities have to include the whole process from planning, prospecting, and contacting to pitching. Good marketing causes prospects to make contact with your company, meaning that they have already 'bought-in' to the idea of using your company and its products.

Good marketing is like pure gold to the salesperson because half the job has been dealt with. Finding the prospect; contacting key personnel; identifying and targeting the need; making the pitch or presentation and commencing early negotiations. Most of the sales process!

So, by the time the prospect makes contact, their need has been pre-qualified, and they have already seen and understood the possibilities involved in working with your company. The job of sales is conveniently limited to clarifying needs and confirming possibilities, 'packaging' them, quoting, negotiating, securing the deal, and then developing the prospect, who has been elevated to the title of customer.

So, here it is:

THE SALIENT SALES PROCESS

While the 'Engagement, Interaction, Transaction and Management' system is clever, I found that it always needed further explanation. The Salient Process is clearer, more easily understood, and implemented. It is a sales process in its simplest form:

1/ PLANNING
2/ PROSPECTING & TARGETING
3/ CONTACTING
4/ PITCHING & PRESENTING
5/ NEGOTIATING
6/ CLOSING/SECURING
7/ MANAGING & DEVELOPING

good marketing brings in the customer at around this point in the process

No two sales follow exactly the same course or pattern. The Salient process is a guide, a template which must at all times be flexible and adaptable. However, as in all stages of the process, preparation, anticipation and some key skills and techniques will assist greatly in achieving the best deal and give you confidence to follow and stick to your objectives.

You may note that the activities 1 to 3, or 4 are about identifying and qualifying the need, while 4 to 7 are about fulfilling the need. Fulfilling the need can also commence earlier, and qualifying can continue much later in the process.

Even with the best and most effective marketing activities in place, you will still meet people who have never heard of you or your business! For this reason, we also need to know how to develop a sales opportunity from scratch. Techniques for achieving this can be found later in the book.

Since marketing and sales need to be combined to be a really effective force in business development, every salesperson should know the fundamentals of marketing. So here is a brief summary of the principles of good marketing.

THE MARKETING PROCESS

As with all project management, every process starts with planning. To create that plan we need to answer 7 basic questions:

- ***Where do we want to go?***
- **Where are we now?**
- ***How quickly do we want to get there?***
- ***What route(s) do we need to take?***
- ***What resources do we need to complete the task?***
- ***What activities need to be undertaken, and in what order?***
- **How do we monitor, review and know when we have finished?**

There are many other questions, but these, to me, are the most essential.

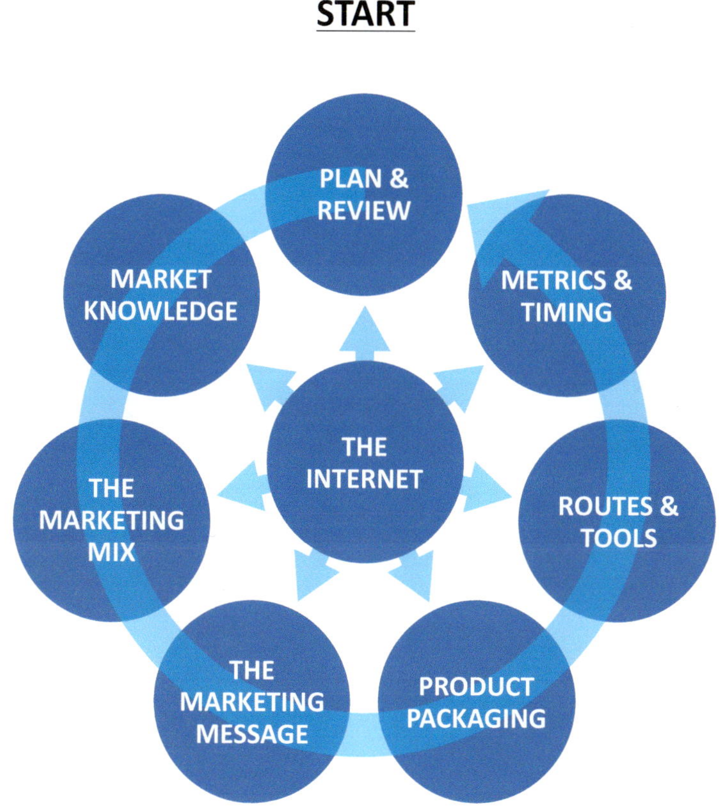

1. To begin, we need...**MARKET KNOWLEDGE**

Identify the prospects that are most likely to want what we offer and who will benefit from purchasing from us.
Without this crucial information we can send quantities of flyers and emails to random people and organisations, in the hope that someone will respond! Clearly, this is unfocussed, expensive and time wasting.

Gather Market Intelligence
Below is a short list of the essentials. Without this basic knowledge, your credibility as a supplier will be difficult to achieve.

The Major Players – (the primary consumers of your Product)
Where do they play? Where can you find them? How can you attract them?

The Competition
Where are they successful? Where (and why) do they fail?

Growing and Declining Sectors
Which are the sectors to target? Which are the sectors to avoid?

Trends and Directions
Where is the market going? How is it changing?

Legislation, Regulation, Accepted Guidelines:
How to remain a respected player?

The Market Size
Is it enough to allow you to grow?

Market Needs
What do you provide that your prospects desperately want?

2. Next, it is important to understand the...**MARKETING MIX**

Also known as THE FOUR Ps which some wag developed into THE SEVEN Ps (apparently, 7 is a magic number) ...

The full pod is: **Product - Price - Position - Promotion**
Plus, the added: **People - Process - Physical Evidence**

The last three are important, but I regard them as implicit in the first four:

Product - Price - Position - Promotion

Defining this little lot is an essential and rewarding activity. Remember that lack of preparation, understanding and belief in any of them will soon be evident to prospective customers and your credibility as a supplier will suffer:

- If you cannot define or explain your **product** and its benefits to your prospect, then you have fallen at the first hurdle.
- If you have set a **price** that does not meet the expectations of the market and your **position** in that market, then very few will pay it.
- If you **position** yourself to target a market sector that is higher or lower than yours, then the offer will not match customer expectations.

If your **product** is a burger served in a lay-by, you are unlikely to target Harrods as a possible customer- the **product** is unlikely to reach their standards; your **pricing** will be lower than anticipated; your reputation (**position**) is unlikely to reach them; and in terms of **promotion** your marketing (a less than glossy flyer) is unlikely to impress.

Equally, if you prepare gourmet dinners (**product**), you are not likely to target motorists as possible customers; the **pricing** to provide a good profit will not suit them; nor will the glossy brochures to **promote** them; and your reputation (**position**) is unlikely to reach passing lorry drivers!

Product, price, position *and* ***promotion*** *need to be considered and defined together and need to match each other and the expectations of the market you have selected.*

YOUR POSITION IN THE MARKET

Where do you position your company?

- As a **high-profile pioneer** which can achieve high profit margins and much success? A good example would be Dyson, the celebrated vacuum cleaner pioneer.

- As a **low profile 'me-too' business** relying on economies of scale, achieving smaller margins and competing on price, while offering other benefits such as speed or availability, but in general can only achieve success by selling in high volume? A good example would be Trumpton Technologies, makers of just one windmill. (Well, have ***you*** heard of them?)

When I first designed a slide for this part of my course, I chose Virgin, another high-profile company for my example. This worked well until I found myself asking the delegates if they aspired to be a Trumpton Technologist, or a Virgin? That evening I changed the slide to Dyson.

BUSINESS PROFILE

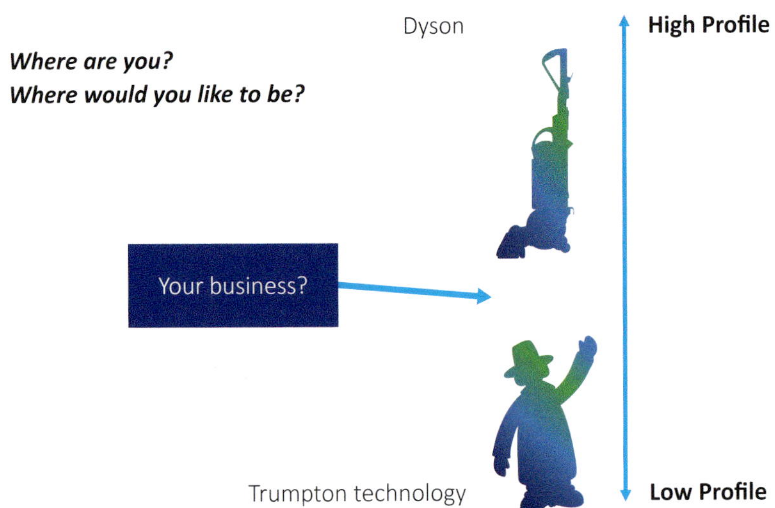

THE OTHER 3PS - People, Process and Physical Evidence

PEOPLE are involved at every stage of the process- your customers and prospects with their wants and needs. It's not about you, your ambition, targets, the wonders of your product, your approach and so on. It's about focussing on your **prospect**.
Focussing on their needs, aspirations, problems and requirements will do much more to help you understand how you can help and as a result, have them buy from you.

PROCESS is important too - by matching your selling process to their **buying process**. If you are doggedly following your own sales or development process, you may be missing an important aspect of selling. Have you made sure that they are ready to buy when you are ready to sell? Sometimes the two don't match which means your expectations and planned cash-flow could be way off-course. For instance, the contact you are dealing with might not be the decision maker, needing to speak to the person that is. Or they might want to pass the idea of the purchase by the person or people who will benefit most from your product - but who are away on holiday.
Knowing *their* process and expected timings will help a great deal. ASK!

PHYSICAL EVIDENCE is about branding – and it's not just about the flyer, brochure or free pen, but the entire package. Consciously, and sometimes subconsciously, we make assumptions and decisions based on how people look, dress, what they drive, how they behave and speak, well before how they are representing their company. In my workshops I sometimes show a picture of a group of salespeople and ask the attendees: *"Which person or persons in the picture would you rather **not** have sell to you?"* After much animated discussion, they choose at least one, some choose more than one, occasionally all of them, but very seldom does someone say, *"none of them".* Those poor salespeople were dismissed out of hand from a photograph.
These types of decisions are often made on a subconscious level within seconds!
Looks, and the way you act matter. Make sure you look and act the part.

The Marketing Mix is important to define and understand, and with this understanding you can devise and develop your **approach** to the market, to your customers and prospects. With a **well-developed approach**, your chance of making a sale is significantly higher. We move from the Mix to the....

3. THE MARKETING MESSAGE

Why should your target market buy your products? What **advantage** can you offer them? What are the benefits of your product? Why buy from you as opposed to anyone else? **Your 'message' should address as many of these questions as possible.**

The **message** is key to the continuity and congruency of your **approach**. I remember when I first started to promote Salient, people would ask me what I did. Generally, my answer was something along the lines of *"Well, I train and coach and mentor in sales, marketing and business development."* Surprise, surprise, they glazed over and switched off. I cringe when I think back. Finally, I started to apply my own teaching (!) and yes, it started to make a good, positive difference. I realised that what my customers and prospects wanted was to *"find more customers and win more sales"* and for many years, that was my attention-seeking mantra, my **big advantage**. Recently, this has changed to *"expertise in growing businesses by securing more sales"* or appropriate variations of this.

AIDA is one of the oldest sales and marketing tools around and still hugely effective. It is also a famous opera by Giuseppe Verdi. It sounds really special to have a name like Giuseppe Verdi doesn't it but translated into English it's just Joe Green! But I digress. AIDA is an acronym standing for: ***ATTENTION - INTEREST - DESIRE - ACTION***

So, how can we apply this to your business?

ATTENTION

We need to attract people's attention. We have 3-5 seconds to attract their attention before they drift off. What can we tell them in 3-5 seconds that will attract their attention?! There is no point in listing features or elaborating on the benefits. However good these are, you will have lost them at number three. Go for the big **advantage**. What major **advantage** can you give them by working with you or buying from you?

- It may be a lifestyle thing where you can give them more time, more comfort or more pleasure.
- It may be financial; more money, more stability, or perhaps more status - more credibility or a higher profile.
- Whatever it is, it needs to be exactly what they want or need and will grab their attention.

INTEREST

Once attention has been truly grabbed, then we look to develop their **interest**.
We do this by describing the many **benefits** that your product and working with you will bring, which might be any or all of the aspects that you don't choose as your main **advantage**. It might be:

- saving time or money or
- helping people to stand out in the market and outshine the competition

DESIRE

While you are describing the **big advantage** and the many **benefits** that you can bring them you are:

- creating in your prospect a DESIRE to do business with you
- building your CREDIBILITY
- developing their COMMITMENT to continue engaging with you

ACTION

Then, it is essential to leave them with a CALL-TO-ACTION. If you don't, it's as bad as the 'no-close'- when you finish by simply saying that they have all the information they need and suggest they get in touch if they are interested!
In written communication, the CALL-TO-ACTION could be:

- Call a number
- Send an email (quoting a reference number so you can track the marketing)
- Complete a questionnaire
- Place the business.

Verbally, it could be:

- Arrange to meet again
- Send some details and follow-up
- Make an introduction

There are many things you can do that will help to continue engagement and develop a relationship.

HOW TO DEVELOP YOUR OWN MARKETING MESSAGE USING 'AIDA'

1/ List all the **benefits** you can think of that your customers will receive when working with you. Select the most powerful as the big advantage. If you cannot decide which is the most powerful or the most needed benefit, why not ask the question? Call or email your best contacts and ask them what they would value most from a supplier such as yourselves.

2/ Consider the **differentiators**- why would they come to you as opposed to your competition? This could be your main advantage, but certainly one of the benefits you offer.

3/ Be prepared to **adapt the message** for different markets, sectors or decision makers (more on this later).

4/ Using pictures, offers, video, guarantees, value statements (17% more - better than...) can all add to the message and help attract attention and develop interest.

Using **AIDA** in this way will help your prospects to understand what you are about and 'where you're coming from', and you will be more likely to persuade them to buy.

AIDA can and should be applied to your 'elevator pitch' in networking (the short answer to the question 'what do you do?') It could also form your main Tag line for the first page of your website, your flyers and business cards. In fact, everything that your prospects will see, or experience needs to display, repeat and reinforce this message.

4. PRODUCT PACKAGING

This is not specifically about the box in which your product or service is delivered.
I refer to the combination or presentation of products or services in a way and at a price which attracts old and new business.

Call a product or service by another name and it may attract new interest. Different names or descriptions will relate to different sectors or groups of people and in doing so, you can attract a whole new market.

If you combine products and/or services and offer these at a special price, then again, some prospects will see and appreciate the extra value this offers.

Packaging in this way can be offered at strategic times in your business:

<u>They can be applied as part of:</u>

- A Contingency Plan – perhaps to overcome a failing initiative
- A Special Offer – to develop short term revenue,
  perhaps there's a dip in the market
- A 'value-added' offer – if extra is needed to win the business, e.g. in negotiation
- A stimulus – a way of reminding past contacts of your existence and to maintain a good profile in the market.

Case Study:

I will, on occasion, present a sales and/or marketing workshop. I had a number of titles to choose having written around six in all over a few years. A few years ago, the interest for these started to wane and instead of the usual minimum of around six or seven delegates, I was receiving only two or three bookings.

I realised I needed to 'beef-up' the package. Two of the most popular titles were, 'Selling Yourself' and 'Smart Networking'. The first acknowledged that people buy from people and unless you could sell yourself as an effective and reliable professional, then you were unlikely to attract those wanting to buy. The second provided useful strategies and techniques for being highly effective and profitable at networking.

Realising that you started by 'selling yourself' in networking situations it made sense to combine these workshops. Offering a small discount for booking both at once, I held Selling Yourself in the morning and Smart Networking in the afternoon. As a package it was easy to see the sense and value in this and bookings increased accordingly.

Introducing new packages during seasonal lulls can turn-round a low-income month and produce record-breaking results.

Careful product/service packaging can make a significant difference to the success of your sales strategies.

5. ROUTES & TOOLS

Once we have devised a powerful message, we need to know how we are going to present it to the market. What routes-to-market will best grab the attention and raise our profile in your chosen markets and sectors. We also need to select the appropriate tools and materials that will help boost our profile and secure a positive response. I could wax lyrical on these but the best way to grasp the concept is to peruse the slide I created for my training courses. Some of the suggestions may not be appropriate for your business, product or market. On the other hand, there could be an aspect which you haven't yet considered, that may help to increase your profile and generate more business.

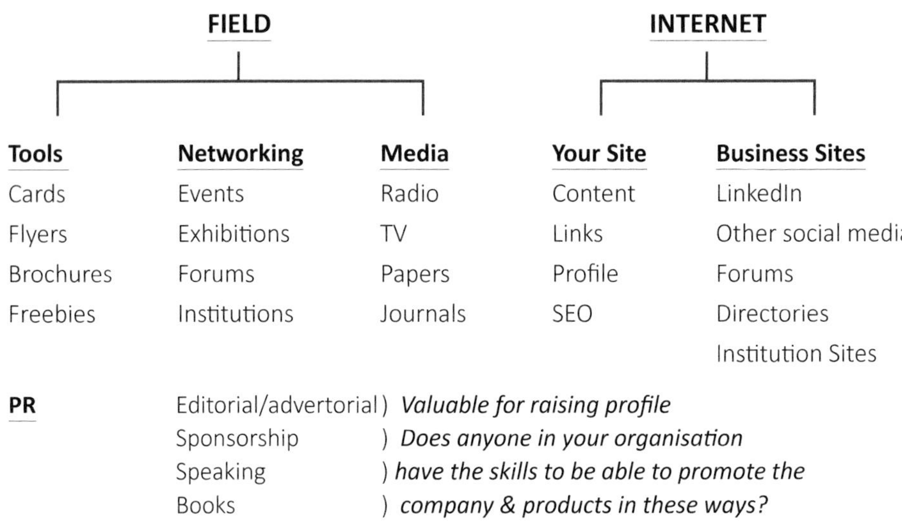

THAT WONDERFUL BUSINESS TOOL - THE INTERNET

Isn't the internet wonderful? So much opportunity, so many prospects, so much rubbish. I do enjoy the fact that you can find out anything at any time and be 95% certain that it is 100% accurate! However, I am concerned that while we have made the pool of knowledge very, very wide, it is no longer deep.

Before the internet, if you needed to be an expert, you used books and periodicals and met with current experts to discover the latest thinking. Your scope was limited, but the depth was much greater. Specialists would know a very great deal about not a lot; a narrow field. Nowadays, 'specialists' don't have to know a very great deal. They just need to know where to find what they need on the internet. This gives people the opportunity to know a little about an awful lot. Hence the knowledge pool has become wide and shallow, compared with the former narrow and very deep pools we used to plunge into. The phrase 'fathom the depths' is now seldom used, whereas 'toe-in-the-water' is more apposite for today's knowledge investigations.

I worry that this situation encourages fast decision making that is not necessarily well researched or well judged. The temptation for any expert in this situation is to take a little information and extrapolate from this. Their expert opinion is not necessarily as sound as it should be and in use, it can produce errors or significant misjudgements.

You may wonder why I placed the internet as the centre circle in the diagram back on page 8. Some may argue that this gives it too much prominence in marketing. Others will say the circle should be bigger because it is the most important part of marketing today. I say it is a useful tool that can be applied to all aspects of marketing to great positive effect.

However, ***ideally***, it needs to be operated alongside other marketing media. Its prominence should be decided when considering the target audience. How much do they use the internet? You must decide yourself its prominence in your business.

SOCIAL MEDIA AND ITS PLACE IN BUSINESS

Used well, social media can be a very powerful tool in business. With careful and considered use it can be invaluable for finding new prospects and opportunities, raising your profile and maintaining business relationships. Unfortunately, it can also be time-soaking, distracting and even misleading.

Regarding internet and social media platforms; you must choose which ones are best for you. You are not obliged to have a presence on every site and doing so is likely to take up a lot of your valuable time. Ask yourself a couple of key questions:

Who are my target customers?
Which site are they most likely to frequent?

Defining the answer to the first question is a must. If you don't know the answer to the second, then take a look and see who is active on the sites and what they do. Alternatively, ask existing customers which is their favoured site; then join it.

Everyone has a point of view when it comes to social media. Often these are very strong views! One marketing expert has told me that Facebook is by far the best as it has a much larger readership than any of the others. I made the point that there may be more readers but are they likely prospects who would be interested in my business? He then announced that the platform had secured significantly more interest than from any other site.

And that's the point. ***It is not how many people read it, but are they my target market?*** It is similar to when you use Google Analytics to interrogate your website. The first level of analysis tells you simply how much traffic you have had, or how many people have looked. But were they your target market? As a fictitious example, you may be a sales lead generation company calling yourself 'Feeding the Pipeline'. Your traffic may be high but how many of these are plumbers who have found you by accident? You may have many website visits, but this is of no use if 90% are plumbers who are not interested in your product or business. Hence:

TIP: Use website analytics, but, delve deeper. Try and find out who visited and from where. You can also find out which pages of your site they read the most; in other words, what product or service they are most likely to want. This is very useful information for structuring, building and growing your business. You may need to pay for this information but the ROI, (the return on investment) will be high. Alternatively, you can pay someone to analyse this for you, and they can help you compose your website to attract the most visits. Look for SEO (Search Engine Optimisation) experts.

Personally (and it often ends up simply a personal preference), I do not use **Facebook** for business. To me, Facebook is designed more for 'gossip'. I use it to find people and maintain contact with my family and friends. I did once have a link to a web designer but started to resent the intrusion, when, in the middle of reading about my family's exploits, up popped an attempt at a quick sale of website services. Some use it for business, but I think it works best for business-to-consumer companies.

I use **LinkedIn** for a more professional approach. There are useful services available, even to non-paying subscribers so I use it to search for personnel in a particular target company, or to tell of my latest blog and provide links to my website for them to read it (and to capture their details.) And I link the blog on my website to **LinkedIn** and **Twitter** to give a more 'rounded' approach!

Now, **Twitter.** Are you a twit? While I am fond of the Business-Bites that I create for my customers, I am not that enamoured with the Twitter approach which is dangerously addictive, invasive and potentially time-soaking. However, I will maintain a presence on Twitter as I do have connections there who are not necessarily on LinkedIn. Other sites, such as **Pinterest** and **Google Plus**, are available. How many do you need?

TIP: If you really want to cover all bases, use one of the social media organizing platforms such as **Hootsuite** or **Buffer**. While they simply spread the same message over multiple platforms, they do it in one button press.

In short, be aware and beware of social media. Even Google uses face to face events to promote their web advertising...think about it! Use social media as one part of your engagement strategy, but don't let it absorb you.

You cannot beat the personal, face-to-face approach when it comes to building real and rewarding business relationships.

As a final story; I quizzed a friend who runs a business around social media. I suggested that in the beginning geeks shouted that we should all use it. Gradually we complied, but not necessarily for the right business reasons – many were simply following it as the latest business 'fashion'. My friend promotes it by saying that we need to use it because everyone else is using it. I challenged him with the thought that that if the main reason we use it is to follow the heard then it has little or no intrinsic value other than the large number of people who have 'signed-up'. He thought long and hard, shrugged, smiled and said, 'Basically, you're right'. In fairness, while it adds little to the engagement, it can help greatly to facilitate it.

Social Media: engage and use it, but be selective, and use it carefully.

My very last word on the internet, I think....

EMAIL MARKETING

This too has its strengths and weaknesses. Its main weakness is that everyone receives barrel-loads of emails a day unless their filters are very strict. If an email arrives at the wrong time, such as in the middle of an important task, conversation, call or meeting, then it will be left for a time. By the time you can get to it, twenty more have come in to distract you further. Spammers are clever and it can sometimes be difficult to spot the difference between important emails and wasteful spam.

On the other hand, if you have built a loyal following, or have a well-chosen contact list, then your credibility will be sufficient that they will open your every missive. The big question is what to do about cold emailing?

COLD EMAILING ('spamming')

I do not promote cold-calling or cold emailing at any time. It has been illegal in the US for some time and now the same applies here in the UK. I have devised many useful ways of making every first contact at least warm, if not roasting. The aim is to have prospects who at least know of you, and who may even be expecting a call. This can be done! Details of these skills and techniques this appear later in the book.

Before we go any further, I have to introduce GDPR and PECR;
The General Data Protection Regulation and the Privacy and Electronic Communications Regulations.

The first covers data management, the second relates to contacting prospects and customers. They are European laws which the UK has adopted and will maintain, whether we are in the EU or not (we are in at the time of writing!) They are there to protect personal data from reaching the unscrupulous or criminal and to prevent the ever increasing and invasive cold calling. I support their introduction as I too am fed up with the bombardment of irrelevant, pressured or even criminal approaches. Such activities do not help those of us who are trying to earn a living by ethical and honest means.

The laws are designed to prevent cold-calling and some cold-contacting. We all suffer from those calls which promote (often unethically) goods or services that we do not need or want. Worse than this (spam), they can be 'phishing calls', whereby they attempt to gain banking details and access to your accounts. However, as with most government initiatives, it was rolled out with insufficient or poorly explained process.

Here are the key aspects:

1/ You are allowed to make contact if you can prove or justify a **'legitimate interest'**. This is reasonably easy to do for Business-to-Business contacts. If you genuinely feel they would benefit from hearing about your product or service, then they could not complain that your contact is spamming.

If you have been sending them information, such as a newsletter, or they have been in contact before and have not requested an 'opt-out' then this reinforces your 'legitimate influence' claim.

2/ You can no longer rely on just offering an '**opt-out**' – the opportunity to decline further contact. You are now obliged to seek an 'opt-in', whereby they have given consent for your contact. The **'opt-in'** can be achieved at first meeting, by asking them. However, it still needs to be in writing, so a follow-up email asking for confirmation of consent by return is needed.

The 'opt-in' can also be a condition of subscription to a newsletter or website. Even if you have achieved an opt-in, every written contact must still include an opportunity to opt-out. This is the part that, unfortunately, many companies and organisations misunderstood. They went ahead and contacted their whole contact list asking for them to opt-in. Many were horrified to find that as a result, they had lost 90% of their contact list, which often included former customers! They need not have done this as the majority, if not all had been contacted by them before and so it would be an acceptable 'legitimate interest'. All that was needed was a group letter or email pointing out the legitimate interest aspect and inviting anyone who no longer wanted to hear from them to opt-out. That way they could have kept around 80-90% of their contacts and caused little or no disruption.

For this reason, Business-to-Consumer contacts are mostly affected. In this situation it is potentially more difficult to prove 'Legitimate Interest'. Some companies still stretch the point; every house has windows therefore there must a be a legitimate interest in double glazing! The best solution for B-to-C companies is to make their marketing so compelling that their prospects contact them directly. I know, 'utopia', but it is a great way of achieving the best turnover and profit.

3/ Lastly, GDPR requires you to have:

- A Privacy Policy
- A Data Usage Policy
- Data held legitimately and securely in one place*
- Registration with the ICO, the Information Commissioner's Office
- Regular reviews of all the above

* This could be encrypted on your laptop and copied to a cloud as clouds have their own protection systems.
I recommend that you either study the requirements on the ICO website and/or seek professional advice from an expert.
Failure to address the above can result in fines from the ICO.

EMAIL CONTENT

In my view, the best emails are not these that cover around 6 pages or want you to scroll down again and again until you give up the will to stay awake. These seem to be favoured by US based sales and marketing companies, and some in the UK who simply copy US business techniques. Unfortunately, more often than not, these include pressure techniques with unreasonable time limits and misleading discounts.

They may provide a useful filter in that only people with the patience to get to the end of the email will have a genuine need for the product. However, in my view, most people do not have the time to read all the reasons why they should buy this wonderful product in one sitting. While it focusses on how good it is, often without telling you what it is, it goes on about how wonderful the product is, that it has helped so many people, that it has transformed the lives of countless individuals, that if you don't get on board you'll be missing out on the deal of a lifetime, and so on. So 'salesy', so ...delete.

I advocate the short, attractive, perhaps intriguing approach. Use sales techniques such as **AIDA** (Attention, Interest, Desire, Action), but keep it short and entice or encourage them to click on a link to find out more. The link should take them to an appropriate page on your website where you can measure and monitor their interest. Now you have filtered out any who are not interested. You could make it just as enticing but leave out the final part of the story and the price. A second link completes the picture and provides them with the means to make a decision and do what is necessary to purchase the product. At each stage you have filtered-out those who are less likely to buy.

At each stage, if you are using analytics effectively, you will know who is still interested. In this way, you will not only secure more business, you will know who reached stage two but hesitated. And they become your next **'hot-target'**.

6. METRICS & TIMING

The term 'Metrics' we use to refer to the measurement of progress. This can be done in many ways, particularly within the disciplines of sales and marketing. Sales has many aspects that can be measured, and this is covered in detail in the next chapter. Marketing also benefits from the measurement and review of progress. A classic example is the request, usually in small type, for the reader to quote the given code when responding to the marketing. In this way, the marketeers can gauge which of their initiatives has worked best. If one marketing initiative achieves significantly more responses than another, then that method and style of marketing is used again, while that which was less successful is shelved.

Without the ability to measure the effectiveness of different marketing approaches, a great deal of time, effort and money can end up being wasted on attempts that prove highly ineffective. At the same time, an initiative proving to achieve great results can be adopted for other campaigns and products.

The **timing** of such initiatives and campaigns needs to be considered carefully too. Introducing a new product or idea at the wrong time of year, if the market is seasonal, can result in efforts being wasted.

If a campaign has been planned involving regular contact, the frequency of that contact can make a significant difference to its success. If the contacts, email, letter or call, are made too frequently, the recipient may feel pestered. Too infrequent and the recipient can forget the content of the previous contact made. The frequency can depend also on the complexity of the content. For instance, a very short 'teaser' may be followed up within a fairly short timescale, whereas a lengthier and involved missive or message may well benefit from longer time gaps to allow the full content to be digested.
As in all these cases, rules of thumb may be used. However, these may differ between markets and product types. It may be safer to try varying the approach, the content and the timing, so that, the results can be analysed and the best and most successful of each chosen for future use.

MARKETING FOR SALES - CONCLUSION

This was a very brief insight into Marketing for Sales, showing the importance and value of good marketing; the options of how to devise and develop the marketing content; the many ways of promoting your message; and useful ideas in making your business that much more attractive. As with every skill and technique described in this book, it is up to you how and how much you adapt and adopt to use in your business.

The application of these skills is often the key to their success, and this is where my courses and sessions prove particularly useful.

In the next section, we will be looking at **Sales Planning**. Again, this will include aspects of managing your sales activities. Good planning makes the sales process far more effective than the 'scatter-gun' or 'build it and they will come' approaches, which are often adopted by less foresighted business people than your good selves!

CHAPTER 3

SALES PLANNING

'55 SHADES OF SELLING'

Let me tell you about a workshop I developed a few years ago. I began to realise that I could not tell people they ***should*** adopt an ethical selling approach as that would be a little contradictory. When it comes to approaching sales and marketing, everyone has to decide for themselves what is ethical, what is cynical manipulation and what is borderline. The workshop was called **'55 shades of selling'** and, for some reason, it proved quite popular.

To try and summarise a morning's workshop into a few paragraphs is not easy, but I will do my best: **In every sale you are seeking to influence the prospect and persuade them to buy from you. You may have many skills in selling but it is how you apply those skills that will have a direct effect on your success, and your job satisfaction.**

So, how do you seek to influence?

At one end of the scale you have Dominant Selling: the infamous 'pushy' or 'pressure salesman'. We have all met them at some time. Sadly, often it was the car or double-glazing salesmen who developed this sort of reputation. Unfortunately, this approach became widespread and the sales discipline itself developed a bad name. Although I believe the situation has improved and people are beginning to stand up for ethical selling, there is still too much of this around.

At the other end of the scale we have Submissive or Benign Selling, where the close is omitted in favour of a request for the prospect to call if interested. Users of this approach can be from any type of business and market. In between those two extremes you will find most other businesses. It is up to every reader and their business to decide what is right and wrong for them and their business. **It is about their motives, their intent and their conscience.**

To help people decide, I introduce them to a series of questions. Some are straightforward, some are easy, some are trickier. How far would you go?!

Are you a manipulator or a by-stander?!

Try answering these questions –

Would you....

- **make every effort to influence the buyer towards favouring your product?**
- **exaggerate your costs to appear to have lower profit and make your price seem more acceptable?**
- **fit your approach and phrasing to match the buyer's interests or background?**
- **mimic and mirror the buyer's actions? (These last two are ideas developed in NLP: Neuro-Linguistic-Programming)**
- **if you are using this sale to achieve a different objective, do you admit to this?**
- **feign interest in the buyer's life, hobbies or grumbles?**
- **attempt to gain (a) favour by 'doing them a favour'?**
- **inflate the selling price then offer a big discount?**
- **undermine the competition in any way possible?**
- **make up statistics to support your claim?**
- **lie, exaggerate or add a positive spin on your abilities, experience, knowledge or connections?**
- **suggest 'scarcity' of your product or invent a time limit for your offer?**
- **do you 'Fake-it 'til you Make-it'?!**

Clearly, some are more difficult to answer than others. The choice is yours entirely. It is down to two important aspects. Your **MOTIVE** and your **CONSCIENCE**. If you apply a 'positive spin' that is one thing, but if you intend to manipulate, add pressure or apply any non-ethical influencing technique, then you alone will have to live with your conscience *and the possible consequences*. I firmly believe that 'truth-will-out'.

DIFFERENT SALES APPROACHES

At one end of the scale you have the 'pushy' salesperson, who will apply pressure techniques to win the business. He may achieve this, but the buyer will not enjoy being pushed or manipulated into buying and so is less likely to place any more business with the salesperson.

At the other end of the scale, you have the 'benign' salesperson, the one who is prepared to say, 'there's all you need to make your decision, if you want to work with us, give me a call'. (Not an acceptable close!) This is most likely to leave the buyer with the impression that the seller is not bothered; not really interested in winning the business.

Ultimately, neither of these are successful as they do not win the respect and trust of the buyer and the sales process is less than enjoyable or fulfilling.

I favour and promote what I call the '**Challenging Sale'**.

The 'Challenging Sale' comes into play when you have attempted to close but have received a negative response.

I believe it acceptable to challenge this 'no' once (or it can be twice if there is no danger of the relationship suffering). To do so will have a number of positive effects:

- It will confirm your commitment and enthusiasm for working with the prospect.
- It will help to draw out the real reason for the 'no' and allow further discussion.
- It will allow a counter-argument to be developed and applied where possible.
- In applying a challenge, it will gain you more understanding and respect from the buyer, increasing your credibility.

The 'no' can be due to budget issues, policy changes, project delays, personnel changes, competition activities and so on. You won't find out unless you ask! Unless you ask or challenge, you will have no more chance to sell to this person. Without a challenge, you have accepted the 'no' and lost the business. With a challenge you have at least one more chance to win the business. This is covered in the later chapters covering **negotiation** and **closing** or securing the business.

If the challenge brings forth a reason for the objection to placing an order, and its origins, then it is likely to be possible for you to overcome the more specific details you have been given.

If you are concerned or nervous about challenging, ***ask their permission***.

'Do you mind if I challenge you?' or *'Do you mind if I just ask you a little about how this came to be a 'no'?'* They are very unlikely to deny you this polite request.
Beware challenging too much as this can easily sour a relationship. I believe a simple, polite request, perhaps a couple of times if necessary, will suffice and give you another chance for the business.

'Pressure selling' is still very common. It is similar to how some politicians and media interviewers behave and, in my view, ***it is nothing short of bullying***. Certainly, it has the same results; those on the receiving end feeling frustrated, cornered, often humiliated and angry. There should be no place in our society for bullies.

Where are you on the scale of ethical/effective selling...what 'shade' are you?

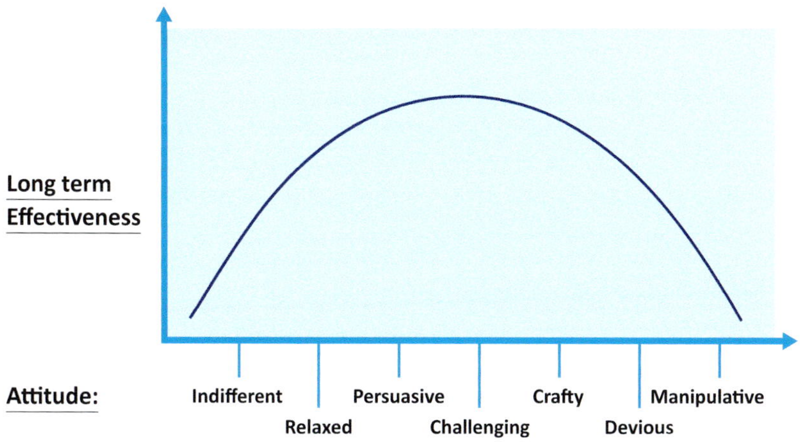

The SALIENT POINTS OF INFLUENCE AND PERSUASION:

- Selling skills are important, but it is how you apply those skills that counts.
- Adding any form of pressure can be seen to change a 'persuasive pitch' into a cynical manipulation.
- Keep asking the questions and keep checking you are engaging with the buyer and fulfilling the need.
- Smile, be enthusiastic, but don't be oppressive!
- Investing time and effort will help to develop their trust and fulfil their need.
- Focusing on mutual benefit will help to ensure a 'win-win' deal.
- Remain consistent and honest as always 'the truth will out'.
- Always, try not to sell to them; instead help them to buy from you
- After a 'no' - make your challenge but be prepared to walk away. There will always be other opportunities. They may even come back to you.

Approaching selling with good intent, wanting to help rather than to sell, will enable you to:

- ***Build lasting, positive and profitable relationships***
- ***Give you more chances to win the business, gain testimonials and referrals, and best of all, more repeat business.***
- ***And, help you to enjoy every sale!***

Now we have our approach, we need to plan.

SALES PLANNING

How do we plan?

There is a widely attributed and much used quotation that goes like this: *'Failure to plan is planning to fail'.* Some still scoff at the trite nature of this, but it is very true, and like all home truths, it is painful to note that too often we fail to plan properly.

There is another one: *'If you don't know where you are going, any road will take you there'.* Again, very true and a classic salient point.

Clearly, planning for sales will make a big difference to achieving our aims and being successful. So, what do we need when planning for sales? We need an overall goal, objectives and targets. Unless we have targets, we will never know if we are 'on-plan'. Unless we measure and compare against target we will not know if we are likely to achieve the target or if we need to be doing more, or even something else.

If we are hitting targets, then we would likely be achieving our objectives. If we achieve our objectives than we would certainly reach our overall goal. Let me explain using the pyramid approach:

The Planning Pyramid

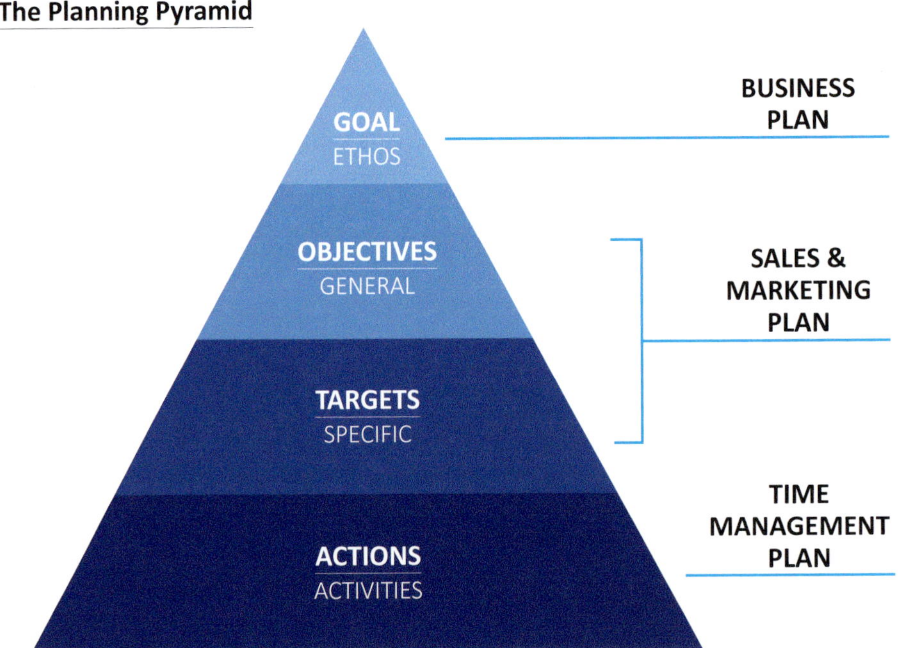

We need an overall **GOAL**, say to become the go-to business for people wanting widgets in the south-west. We can also add in that we want to reach a turnover of £50M* within 12 years. You can also introduce the basic ethos or character of your company here by adding something along the lines of '...and be known as the best supporting supplier in this field'.
* Please insert the appropriate figure for your plan!

Once the goal is set, then we can consider the **OBJECTIVES**. While still fairly general, these start to add specific aims to the mix, with ideas to become the biggest widget supplier in the county within 3 years and to achieve turnover of £5M by next year, £20M by year five and so on.

To achieve these objectives, we need to set specific **TARGETS**. The detail is up to the individual, but it can be anything and everything from annual, quarterly or monthly targets of turnover or of winning strategic customers, the level of your business profile, or perhaps the level of repeat business. However, you decide to measure your success, plan for it and measure your progress towards it.

In order to keep these in focus, it is essential to have these written down. As the drawing shows, the goal needs to be stated in the **BUSINESS PLAN**; a document of any length between 1 and around 12 pages (+appendices), outlining theses specific and overall aims. Business plans are useful for focusing on the main reasons and desires for being in the business, your business, and writing it can be an art. On the other hand, some say, other than in its shortest form, it is an unnecessary document.

The objectives form the main part of the **SALES & MARKETING PLAN**, with the specific targets detailed and added as forecasts in the appendices. This plan is key to the business growth and details strategies for enabling that growth and development.

The activities needed to achieve the targets need to be listed and included in your **TIME MANAGEMENT PLAN** which gives timings and milestones for all the activities needed to achieve them. With some time allocated to each activity, these can be scheduled into every week or month as needed.

So, we have targets, objectives and our overall goal. How do we apply all this to our business? Take a look at this:

The Planning Triangle

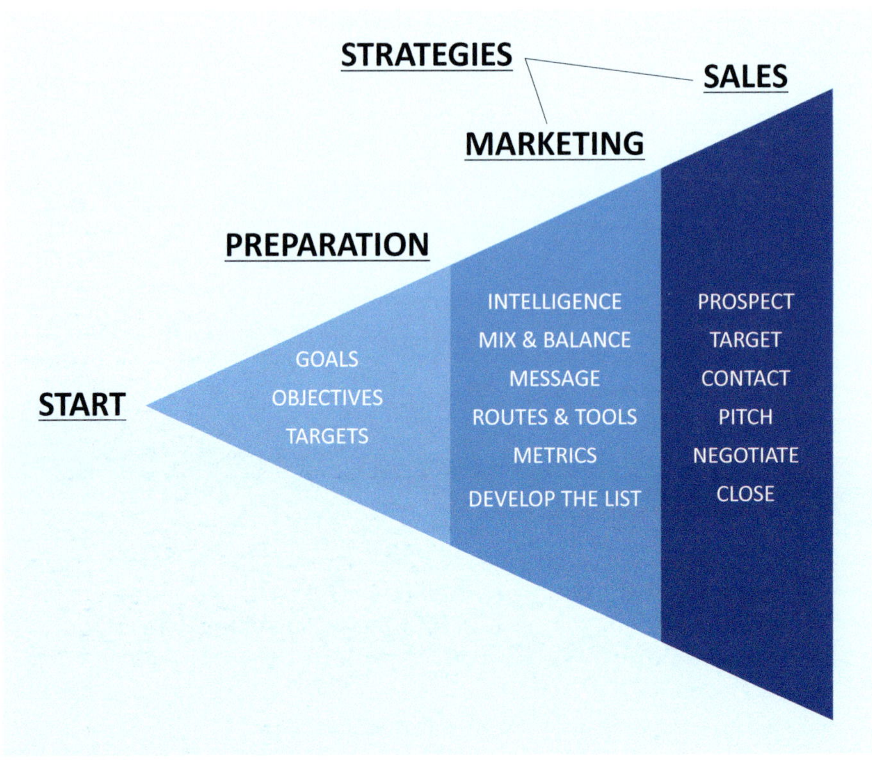

Once you have set the goals, objectives and targets, you need some way, some system or process to achieve them. Set up and implement some marketing strategies and initiatives, as described in the previous sections. Use the marketing intelligence and feedback to start selecting your list of suspects, qualify them as likely to be interested in you and your products and select your first 'hot list' of prospects. This is the part of the process known as **prospecting** and is covered in more detail in the next section of the book, as are the subsequent stages of **contacting, pitching, negotiation and closing**.

As we have seen before, it does not stop there. To provide a full picture of the planning process, customer management or 'client development' needs to be included. *See next page...*

The Complete Planning Triangle

The WHEN is now!

We have looked at the preparation, marketing and selling stages and now need to consider what to do with them once we have welcomed them as a customer. The list under the heading 'Management' is not set in stone and can be changed to suit your approach, but it does include some important aspects of client development. All these are covered in more detail in future chapters, but there are a few points that could be well made at this time.

The FOLLOW-UP is one of the most important, but first-forgotten activities in sales and marketing. A written follow-up of every 'phone call, every meeting, every single contact made, will help to ensure that nothing is missed, nothing forgotten, and nothing changed during the sales process.

Usually in the form of an email, ideally with a read-receipt confirmation, it should follow the lines of:

> *'It was good to talk with you again; we covered points A, B and C and agreed actions D (for me to do) and E For you to complete, before we speak again in x weeks' time. If you understood it differently, please respond by return, otherwise I look forward to speaking with you then.'*

Or words to that effect.

It is the most important tool for managing expectations, controlling and/or leading the process.

LOYALTY DEVELOPMENT can be illustrated with the **'Loyalty Ladder'**:

Customer – you achieve the first sale

Prospect – you confirm the likelihood of their interest

Suspect- you suspect they may have an interest

This is explained in more detail in my next book which covers Client Management and Development. However, it is worth noting that the higher you can move a business relationship up the ladder, the greater the chance you have to receive repeat business; win new business from them; receive a good testimonial; obtain referrals and secure a good base of existing and happy customers.

REFERRALS & TESTIMONIALS are very valuable, but often forgotten by salespeople who are too eager to move on and find new business. These two aspects of relationship building can be very profitable.

Testimonials:
You are likely to find that your own marketing or sales pitch, i.e. anything said or published by you and your company will be regarded with some scepticism, and not necessarily total credibility. Suspicious prospects will think 'well they would say that wouldn't they, after all they are paid to say that'.

However, *if your customer says it*, then their credibility with the prospect will be higher, often significantly so. Your customers are perceived to have no axe to grind and so prospects will take more notice of them. Anything positive that the customer can say or write about you will be hugely valuable to you and should form much of your marketing and selling approach.

Referrals:
Likewise, these are worth their weight in gold. It is much easier to be able to contact a new prospect if you can say 'person x' recommended that I give you a call. Your credibility will be established before you have even started your pitch.
Personal recommendations and referrals are priceless and should be sought and used at every opportunity.

CONTINGENCIES are needed for every eventuality. From my experience, few companies actively consider and develop contingency plans. As a result, they are caught out whenever something unexpected happens that affects their plans.

Contingency Case Study:

As an illustration, a Sales & Marketing Manager and team decide to focus their efforts in a particular market sector. They devise tailored marketing, directed specifically at the users and decision makers in that sector (and therefore, would be unlikely to attract businesses in other sectors).

Unfortunately, and without warning, legislation is brought in that makes it impossible for most people to use the company's products. (An alternative scenario could be that their largest target suddenly pulls out of that sector.) Anyway, for whatever reason, the chances of achieving the plan are now zero. Without a plan B contingency plan, it may be another 6 to 12 months before a new sector can be targeted effectively. Clearly targets will be missed by a mile and the continued existence of your company may be put at risk. However, a plan B would have been at least part-prepared, allowing the delay to be shortened to manageable levels. Plan Bs should be simple, quick to bring to market and be of known value to your prospects and customers.

Salient Case Study:

Following my own advice, I had developed a contingency plan. In late 2015, I had five large companies asking for proposals for Salient to provide them with Technical Sales Training. All was going well, and my proposals had been well received. Then nothing happened. The original Brexit vote was looming large. After much chasing and discussion with my prospects, it became apparent that they wanted to 'wait-and-see' what the economy was going to do after the vote. Unfortunately, in this country, training is regarded as a luxury not a necessity(!) and so it becomes one of the first thing to cut back in a crisis. Over just a few weeks, these five companies pulled out of discussions and my cash-flow and turnover forecasts suddenly looked very poor.

Luckily, I had a Plan B. If the large companies were no longer active, the smaller companies had to continue to survive. I developed the 'One-to-One Coaching Day'. This was a loss-leader, intended to:

A. Fill the financial hole (at least partially)
B. To provide opportunities for developing new customers at the lower end of the market (to cross-sell and up-sell)

It was intended to be a 'special offer' for just one month. I introduced this to my networking friends and had 15 of them book a coaching day in the first two weeks. They paid a fraction of the income expected from the corporate companies, but there were enough of them to enable me to keep going. It became so popular that I continued the offer month after month. It was hard work, but the returns were very good and in around 18 months I had over 80 days booked. Now that was a successful contingency plan!

Whenever possible, have a plan B ready.

The EXTRA-MILE is worthy of its own section and is covered in detail in my next book.

The BOSTON and ANSOFF MATRICES are useful tools for business development and worthy of the lengthy description given to them, again in the next book which covers all matters relating to customer development. The first relates to your existing customer base and allows easy identification of those customers that are ideal for targeting for growth, and those you may consider reducing your level of involvement.
The second is a simple visual representation of product and market development and diversification.

NEW MARKETS - An important activity of sales management is to extend and grow their markets. The manager and the team should always be on the lookout for new applications and new potential areas of interest for their products or services. Developing new markets is often hard and time-consuming work. However, the rewards can be significant. Pioneering new markets, allows you to be 'first-in'; ahead of the competition. You can be the established market-leader long before the competition catches up!

MONITOR AND REVIEW - How do you know where you are against plan, or know if you are successful if you fail to measure, monitor and review your progress? We have looked at metrics in the marketing section, noting the value of measurement, analysis and its application to management of marketing. Metrics prove to be even more important in the sales discipline as there are far more things that can be measured, and which will benefit from the analysis and application of the results.

'If you can't measure it, you can't improve it': Lord Kelvin

Here is one of the few pieces of jargon that I use regularly: KPI is one of the dreaded TLAs; Three Letter Acronyms, and it refers to Key Performance Indicators. In simple terms, these are the criteria by which you wish to measure performance. Here are a few examples:

Suggested Choice of KPIs

- Turnover
- Costs
- Profit
- Product Enquiries
- General enquiries
- Internet 'hits'
- Website subscribers
- Marketing success
- Conversion rates, for converting – Contact to enquiry
  - Enquiry to sale
  - Quotation to sale
  - Customer to client (repeat business)
- Repeat business value
- Inward/outward calls
- Complaints

As you can see, there are many ways of measuring progress and success. Some of these will be appropriate to your business, some may be less so. Choose your KPIs wisely and it will become much easier to:

a) Know where you are against plan
b) Know where to do more to improve
c) Know what and when to change
d) Manage the key activities

How can we monitor, review and manage these KPIs? There are many business tools that can be considered, from a simple monthly forecast of orders received, to a more complex spreadsheet or system that relates costs to overheads and measures these against income and/or profit. Other metrics will consider team or individual activities to be able view performance for each person, territory or product.

It is worth investigating the suitability of Pert Charts, Gantt Charts and CRM systems for your business. An internet search will show these visual aids and you can select the type that suits you, your data and your business.

The chosen metrics are invaluable when managing the sales effort, but caution is needed as 'analysis paralysis' is all too common, particularly in larger organisations.

In the past I have worked for too many companies that relied on up to the minute forecasts and reports, to the extent that at least a quarter of my time was spent in writing and revising these documents. Some was necessary; a lot was time wasted. This proved at least frustrating and often demoralising. The first rule of KPIs is keep it simple! Agreeing regular but not intrusive review meetings and reporting needs will ensure that as much time as possible is allowed for the sales effort to continue, while providing sufficient information for the effort to be managed effectively. This is a tricky balance that will likely require much adjustment before the optimum is reached.

Over 20 years in the field, I became a (reluctant) expert in forecast writing and structure. I devised many of my own rules for the good management of sales metrics and these could easily become the subject of a separate book. However, there is much more to come from the sales process itself, so let's move forward.

TIMING plays a key part in the measurement of the sales effort. When monitoring sales initiatives such as sector targeting, product promotion or other marketing initiatives, Pert or Gantt charts can prove useful. These are more for project management per se but can be applied easily to any such activity. I suggest you interrogate the net to find out more about these management tools.

TIP: Many are good at planning a project or activity with a deadline, a finish-by date. However, and sadly more common, not many remember to schedule a START DATE. Without this, the decision to complete in 4 weeks can result in distraction and a delay in starting. Clearly, this results in a 4-week project being crammed into 3 weeks, causing lower quality results, mistakes, frustration and demotivation. Alternatively, it can result in the full 4 weeks being taken and a week's delay in delivery, causing upset clients or bosses.

Don't forget a start date! *(A tip from our Time Management course)*

CELEBRATE SUCCESS! Finally, I urge you all to celebrate. If you measure, monitor and review effectively, at some stage you will meet or exceed your planned performance.
Celebrate it! It could be something as simple as a choice snack, cakes in the office, a meal, a gift, even a holiday!

If we don't, then what incentive do we have to meet or exceed our planned performance? Human nature says that a prospect who enjoys buying from you, will want to buy more.

Likewise, if you are sufficiently successful and celebrate the results, then you will want to repeat this on a regular basis! It builds job satisfaction, motivation and enthusiasm for doing the job effectively and successfully.

MORE SALES TOOLS:

We have looked at the Salient Planning Pyramid and Triangles and we have seen how customer loyalty can be developed by following the Loyalty Ladder. How do we deduce how many new customers we need or how many new and existing customers we need to approach to achieve our objectives and targets? We use the that old favourite, the 'Sales Funnel'. First we need to define 'conversion rates':

Conversion Rates are a measure of our success in converting prospects into customers. What I call the Primary Conversion Rate is the ratio of achieved customers to prospects contacted. As an example; we may win 1 new customer for every 10 prospects we contact. Our primary conversion rate would then be 1 in 10. You can also work out the conversion rates for every part of the sales process, as shown below:

The SALES FUNNEL

To answer the important question:

How many contacts do we need to make,
in order to have a good chance of achieving our targets?

Before we can deduce this, we need to ask ourselves three important questions:

- What is our target figure for the year in terms of turnover?
- What is the average 'spend' of our customers?
- What are our Conversion Rates?

Without these figures it will be impossible to achieve accurate results in this exercise.

If necessary, make an educated guess.

How to use the Sales Funnel effectively:

The next example shows how decisions can be made with the careful use of known statistics- Average Customer 'Spend' and Conversion Rates- that will have impact on how widely we market our products, how much time we spend prospecting and contacting, and how much effort we put into developing successful contacting strategies.

Example: Let us make it easy for ourselves to illustrate the point. Say, the target turnover is £120,000 (it could just as easily be £1,200 or £12M)

1/ What does our average customer spend? (Say £5000)[1]

2/ Therefore, how many new customers do we need to find to achieve this? £120,000/£5,000 = 24

The next bit depends on your sales process, but if it matches mine:

3/ What is your conversion rate of proposal/quote to winning the order? (Say 1 in 2)[2]

4/ Therefore, you need to have submitted 24x2 = 48 proposals in order to achieve 24 new customers and £120,000 of new turnover.

5/ How many prospect meetings result in a request for a quote/proposal?
This is another conversion rate. **(Say 1 in 3)**[3]

6/ Therefore, you need to have met with 48 x 3 = 144 potential customers to achieve 48 proposal requests and win 24 new customers each spending £5,000.

7/ How many new contacts do you have to make in order to be invited to 144 meetings? This is your conversion rate for contacts to meetings. **(Say 1 in 5)**[4]

Therefore, in this example, you need to have contacted 720[5] new prospects to be in with a chance of achieving your target of £120,000 of new turnover.

Focussing on those figures in red, you could take measures to:
1. Increase the average customer spend, perhaps by cross-selling or upselling. This would reduce the number of new customers needed to achieve the target.
2. Incentivise or make your proposals more attractive in order to improve your chances of winning the business and so increase the conversion rate.
3. Improve your selling skills so that your meetings result in more proposals/quotes being requested.

4. Make your initial contact method more attractive and likely to result in a meeting.
5. Formulate some lead generation strategies that will introduce you to more prospects.

Each of the above figures and ratios demonstrate ways of making significant improvements to your turnover, e.g. in 2. Above, if we can improve our quotations so that we win 3 out of four of them, then we are winning 75% of them instead of 50%. So, if we present 48 proposals, we will win 36 instead of 24; an increase of 50% in turnover!

This is a very powerful approach for increasing business levels.

...and, as an additional income:
As with the case study above, you too could add value to your business by including appropriate 3rd party products bought directly from your website. This could provide further background income to allow even greater business growth.

Case Study:

To some, this is a very sobering exercise. I introduced this process to someone who had been a director in a large organisation but had moved on to set up his own business involved in specialist lighting. The result was that he needed to contact something over 3000 potential prospects in order to reach his target. Simply, there were not enough hours in the day to come close to this figure.
All is not lost in such a situation. What can be done?

In this case I advised him to find a complimentary product to his and negotiate with the manufacturer to enable him to sell this on his website. His customers were happy to find both products in one place and the extra sales changed the figures sufficiently enabling his business to become viable.

The SALES TIMELINE

Finally, we ought to apply the Sales Timeline to this exercise.

Question: in order to achieve your target of £120,000 of increased turnover this year, what should be our monthly target?

Answer: from my experience, most will plump for the simple £10,000 per month.
However, therein lies a problem, because the real world does not work like that.
Let me explain by, again, asking a two key questions:

1/ Is this £120,000 banked, invoiced or order value received?
i.e. have you considered the payment terms offered (30 or 60 days)? Or perhaps the building/assembly/packing/delivery of the product or service? How long is it likely to take between receiving the order and receiving money for delivered product or service? This could be anything from a few weeks to a few months.

2/ From starting to prospect new customers, how soon do you expect the first orders?
i.e. you are very unlikely to win orders in the first month, especially if you are targeting new markets. It can be as much as three or more months before the first order is received.

Taking these two situations into account, what you thought was going to be a new business monthly target of £10,000 has doubled suddenly to £20,000 a month. A sizeable and sobering difference that needs to be considered when 'feeding the pipeline' with regular new business and achieving steady cash-flow.

As my former mentor loves to quote and is illustrated below:

'Turnover is vanity, profit is sanity and cash is reality'.

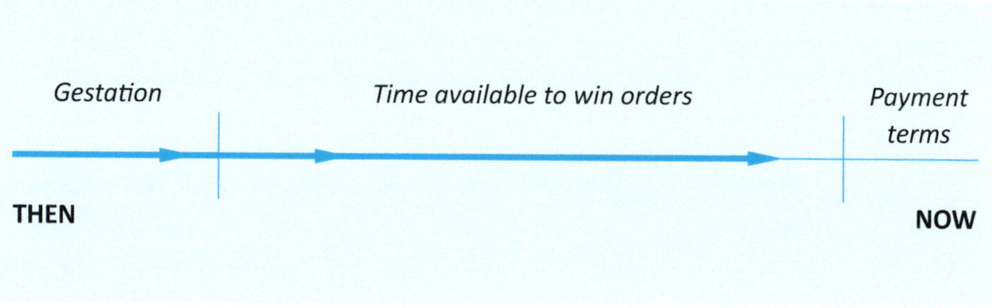

I hope that this section has shown the necessity and importance of good planning in sales and marketing. Sadly, few companies will embrace and accomplish half of these ideas, strategies or techniques. When difficulties arise, those businesses are the ones that will flounder and even disappear.

In Summary:

Good, flexible, timed and measured planning will help to ensure that growth can be maintained and developed without interruption. It will give you the best chance of meeting and exceeding targets. Most of all, it will give you the job satisfaction of seeing your success and of knowing that, whatever happens, you have plans in place to deal with it.

Good sales planning will help to protect against:

- Market fluctuations or downturns
- Loss of key customers
- Loss of key personnel
- Supply problems
- Quality issues
- Cash-flow issues
- Competition activities and growth

Take some time to plan, measure and manage, and give yourself the best chance of success.

So far, we have looked at **Marketing, Sales Approaches** and **Sales Planning**. The next section involves the first stages of putting these plans into action. We have defined our product, our price, target position and developed our marketing messages. We have chosen the first sectors to approach and planned our sales strategies with timings and targets.

Now, we will consider prospecting, commencing with how to develop lists of **hot targets**- companies that have heard of us, know something of our products and services, and will welcome our first contact.

And so, to the joys of prospecting..........!

CHAPTER 4

PROSPECTING AND TARGETING

When I started in my first job as a 'Sales & Marketing Executive', I was given three things: a box of brochures, an industry directory and a telephone. In those days, that was all that I needed to undertake marketing, a little planning, prospecting and contacting! I proceeded to look through the directory, made a list of likely suspects and worked through the list, calling each in turn to see if they had a need I could fulfil. In those days, most people would answer their 'phones and respond to contact requests. I think it is fair to say that things have changed a bit since then.

As we have seen, marketing has become a much broader subject, with many more methods of identifying new prospects. Often there is more than one likely point of contact, and more than one method of making that contact.

Even if you are satisfied with the current level of enquiries, you would be wise to continue 'feeding the pipeline'. However, while it is easier to identify prospective customers, it is somewhat more difficult to identify and make contact with the appropriate personnel. Identifying the ideal target contact is much trickier and making contact on the first attempt is quite rare.

There are three parts to this process: **Prospecting, Analysis and Targeting.**

Part 1: PROSPECTING

It will be assumed at this stage, that goals, objectives and targets have been set and the sales funnel and timeline have been applied so that the amount of new business needing to be targeted and the number of new business opportunities needing to be identified have been decided. Good.

I would also hope that you have defined the ideal customer and their likely need, and confirmed that you have the means to match and supply this need? Excellent. You know how many new opportunities you need and, using the sales funnel, you know how many contacts you are likely to need to be able to achieve that figure. So now we now want to make a list of suspects, or, preferably prospects. Where and how do we find them?

The key questions in prospecting are:

What are you looking for?

How are you looking for new business at the moment?

How do you go about finding your next ideal customers and clients?

How do you find and select your new target businesses?

I am guessing you will be talking to contacts, perhaps networking, searching the internet, perhaps reading the industry/trade/professional journals? Perhaps you are... *'Cold-calling' or Spamming?* You are? Are you meeting the requirements of PECR? If not, we can soon remedy that!

How many prospects do you select before you make contact?

Do you find one and contact them straight away or do you add them to a target list and then schedule some time 'later' to get in touch?

Are you comparing how many contacts you make with how much business you achieve by contacting in that way? (Your Primary Conversion Rate)

Could you prospect differently, find better targets and maybe convert more of them into business?

There are many ways of prospecting and of 'systemising' your prospecting, but some will work better for you than others.

Tip: Ideally, your customer base should be a good balance of:
Existing Customers: *providers of stability and the 'bread and butter' business*
New Customers: *your passport to future growth*

Try this two-stage approach:
1/ Consider Your Existing Customers! No cold calling needed here, and no need to worry about falling foul of GDPR/PECR. Selling to your current customer base is easier by far than starting afresh with new prospects, as they know and like you already (or at least accept you!) and are aware of the quality of your products and services.

If you have forecast a dip in your sales turnover or income, then it will be far quicker and easier to look to existing customers than to find, contact, pitch, negotiate, and close with a new prospect.

If you don't have such a dip, it is still important to make sure you have harvested every opportunity from every existing customer. Can you cross-sell or up-sell? Will they buy more, look for other interested parties within their company, or even consider targeting their competition?

a) **Cross-selling** is when you can offer other products or services that may compliment or are additional to what the customer has identified as a need and has bought already.

b) **Up-selling** is when you can show them the benefit of purchasing the 'next-grade-up'. They may have purchased the 'Bronze Level' of product or service, but they may be persuaded to purchase the 'Silver or Gold Level' as it has so many more bells-and-whistles. Defining a need for bronze but ending up selling silver, or even gold is a real possibility. Always try; you may be pleasantly surprised!

c) **Try for more** because they may simply want more of what you have or are happy to order the next batch or follow-on product. You will never know unless you ASK!

d) **Use your 'Approved Supplier' Status**: If your customer is part of a large organisation, find out, and ask, if other departments, divisions or sites may be interested in what you offer. As an existing and accredited/approved supplier, it will be much easier and cheaper for other parts of the same company to use your products. Costs of trials and approvals will have been covered already by the original user within the group.

e) **Always ask for Referrals:** Have you ever wanted to manage a sales force that costs you nothing? Your customers can be your unpaid sales force! If they have appreciated your strengths and products, then they will be happy to recommend you to their contacts. The questions to ask are:
Who do you know who could also benefit from working with us?
Would you be happy to recommend us?

A good referral is worth its weight in gold as it will ensure that your contact with the new company will be expected and appreciated and you will have built-in credibility, courtesy of your happy customer.
You should also request a testimonial which is used to great effect in marketing to increase your credibility.

NB, all contacts made following referrals will help in GDPR/PECR compliance as the legitimate interest is confirmed by a third party.

f) **Try their Competition:** Unless you have an exclusive agreement in place, the likelihood of their competition needing the same or similar product, is very high. The downside here is the need for discretion and confidentiality. It can be easy to forget which client you are talking to, opening the possibility of giving away company secrets or intellectual property to the competitor. Concentrate! Be careful or avoid completely!

2/ New Customers (ensuring all data/contact regulations rules are followed, (see pages 20-21) Selecting and targeting new sectors and new prospects.

Who else could use my products and services and where will I find these new prospects?

Use your experience, market knowledge and sometimes creativity. Have you been thorough in seeking referrals from existing customers? A referral is often the most effective way of finding new business.

a) Lost Business: (this fits the 'legitimate interest' criteria for the regulations.)

This approach is almost as useful as targeting existing customers. They know of you already, and as long as you have not upset them in any way (you lost the business for good reason), then they will be happy to consider you again.

Even with the wonderful Salient Sales System, you will not win every opportunity! You will win more, but realistically, not everything. But in the unlikely event you receive a 'no', I would hope that you asked all the right questions and did your level best to turn the 'no' into a 'yes'? This is covered in more detail in the chapter on Negotiation, but essentially this is the approach:

'Could you tell me what stopped us winning your business?'
'If we corrected/changed that, would there be an opportunity for you to change your mind and place the business with us?'
'Can you give me a little time to see if I can make those changes?' (and possibly offer some added value).

This can work, so you must at least try! If they say 'no' again, at least you will have done everything possible to win the business or what needs to be changed for another time. If truly lost, then add them to the lost business list, for a re-visit in the future.

When did you last look in your 'lost business' file?
It is quite possible that things have changed in some way with these former prospects.

- Perhaps the supplier they chose has not impressed.
- Perhaps they have had a change of personnel and any links to former suppliers have been severed.
- Perhaps you have since developed new products or a new approach that will impress them this time.

Whatever the reason, some of your work has already been done- they know you and much of what you do. Unless you have upset or disappointed the contact in any way previously, (and even then, the opportunity is still worth pursuing, as above) this could be a comparatively easy route to new business.

b) New Market Sectors:

The Supply Chain Approach

First look at the suppliers and customers of your existing clients – the businesses that already supply to your existing markets. The same can be done with your customers' customers; those they supply to. This link can be used like a referral. We have spoken of the value of referrals and this is another area where you can mine referrals. Your customers have contacts in this area of 'un-tapped' businesses.

The Creative Approach

Other market sectors. Try and think 'out of the box'. Be a bit creative. Choose a completely new but possible sector and target customers that fit your 'ideal' size and market position.

If you can see a possible advantage in their using you and your products or services, then work through an example in preparation for making contact.

If you can write, draw or somehow demonstrate this advantage, then you have created your own opportunity. Try and identify a target person who may use or benefit from your product or service. The result will be your becoming 'designed-in' or the exclusive supplier; an enviable position. (See the next section on Targeting).

The Competition Approach

a) *Your* Competition: Take a look at those sectors and companies that your competitors are servicing. As above, it may be that personnel changes or lack of contact from the competitor may have weakened or even soured their relationship. If open to the suggestion, these prospects will have already decided that your products are of the type they need and will understand your approach.

b) *Your Customer's* Competition: This can be a profitable route to new business, but it can be tricky.

The Pros:

1. They will understand the fit and benefit of using products and services such as yours and so the approach and pitch will be easier.
2. They are likely to know and have seen how your products have helped their competition.
3. Once you have two customers from the same sector, others will follow.

The Cons: (suggesting caution)

1. They may be suspicious of your discretion, or possible lack of it.
2. They may talk to you, only to try and find out what their competition are up to.
3. You may find it difficult remembering which ideas came from which company and so risk being indiscreet with both.
4. Played carefully, this can be a very profitable route to finding more customers.

The above are proven techniques that will help you to put together a list of potential prospects, or 'suspects' as we call them at this stage. Once they have reached this point, many businesses will start 'cold calling' at the top of list and working down. This is demoralising and counter to the new regulations. **There is a better way!**

Part 2: THE PROCESS OF ANALYSIS

List 1: The Big One!

Using a simple spreadsheet, or, if we are talking thousands of companies, some form of CRM system on which we can list all 'suspects', wherever we may have found their details (see below for ideas on how to do this.)

(CRM - Customer Relationship Management System – useful for extracting types of opportunity, values, dates, applying markers and using them to prompt responses etc. These can be free but limited, or they can cost an annual fee and/or running costs but can be valuable if your business warrants it.)

This list can be of tens, hundreds or even thousands of company details. It may be tempting to start at the top and work your way down. DON'T! This may achieve results, but will not be time effective:

- You may find no interested parties in the first 100 contacted – demoralising
- It may take you weeks to find more than 10 who are available to talk – ditto
- By the time you reach 100 contacted, you will have forgotten some that needed following up that you contacted earlier in the exercise.
- With this list you may end up breaking PECR rules.

The large list of 'suspects' is likely to consist of 'cold-contacts'. As we said, this is a demoralising approach, so why not turn these 'suspects' into genuine 'prospects' and reduce the number to manageable levels? So, we are going to turn The Big One into The Hot One by using the following process:

Applying your own criteria:

- start to select companies that are the most likely to need what you have
- those who will understand and value your proposition
- those which are in a serviceable geographical area for you
- and those which are growing in the markets you have chosen to target

Clearly, by undertaking this, you are selecting the best prospects on whom you can do a much more thorough job and are turning a cold Big List into a shorter Hot One!

LIST 1: THE BIG ONE!

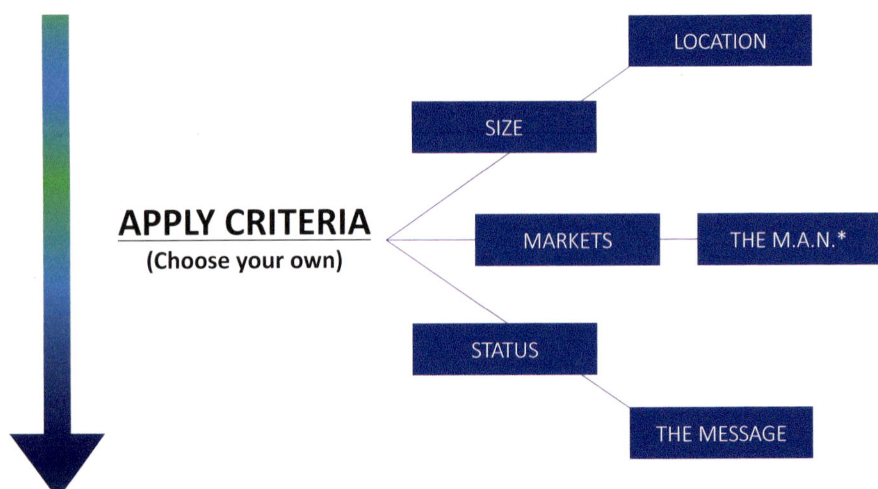

LAST LIST: **THE HOT ONE!**

* **the Money, Authority, the Need**
NB. This is often three different people

Having identified the most likely candidates for contacting, your next 'big spenders', you can justify any 'legitimate interest' query. We can make the list even warmer by 'seeding the market':

Send the contacts you have short-listed some form of marketing. This could be a newsletter, an offer, an introductory letter; anything you can do to make sure that they have at least heard of you before you finally make contact. Ideally, you should mention you will be calling. In this way, ***you need never 'cold call' again***, as they will be expecting your contact, or at least appreciate that it is appropriate for you to call.

While this process is not infallible, you are after all making some assumptions about the suspect - it does improve the efficiency of contacting people and reduce the effort, time and stress involved in cooler or cold calling.

As a further precaution when making contact and to meet regulations, you should always include an option to opt-out. If they do opt-out, then you have filtered the list and you do not need to waste a call. If they do not opt-out, effectively you have their permission to make further contact. Bingo, a hot contact!

The '5 at a Time' Approach

Finally, take your new sorted and filtered list of Hot Prospects and prepare to start contacting. I advocate taking no more than five at a time. These can be managed very effectively with absent contacts recalled, follow-ups done properly, and relationships commenced, all within the space of a couple of weeks.

At the end of the 5-company approach, you will have identified:

- Some for shelving (to be revisited at a later date perhaps)
- Some for re-contacting on an agreed future date ('not now, but call us in ...')
- Some who have shown promise and have agreed to a meeting

Then, move onto the next 5 prospects on the list, and so on.

Once you have achieved sufficient interest and have booked a number of meetings over the next few weeks, you may want to pause in the contacting activity.
Managing your time is very important, as you may end up generating so much interest that you may not have time to follow-up effectively. The lack of proper customer service in developing business is definitely counter-productive. Pace yourself!

Tip: This Hot List must remain a living document. You should be adding to it constantly as new leads are uncovered by, for example:

- referrals from successful contacts
- from colleagues
- from periodicals

If you have contact details that are new, contact them as a priority, particularly if they are a referral – do not let the contact go cold, or even disgruntled!

That, in a nutshell, is the process for making an ideal list ready for contacting.

Part 3: TARGETING

Tip: Before you make a call to ask for the contact's name, be ready with your opening pitch as they may also be willing to put you through. (See the Contacting chapter that follows). Be ready to justify your 'legitimate interest'.

Identifying Your Target Contact

THIS is where the internet comes into its own! If you cannot find the right person by calling the company, use one of the internet business or social platforms.

LinkedIn.

Contacts made through LinkedIn comply with GDPR/PECR. In signing up to Linked In you have joined a 'business club' and therefore have effectively given your permission to be contacted by other members. However, an option to opt-out is still required.

Even with the free membership option, you can find who is listed by writing the company name in the search envelope at the top of the page. The right-hand column then gives you the number of employees listed. Click on the number and it lists these people, giving their job titles and where they are based. In most cases, it will give a photograph, but too often these are not the most professionally produced!
There is also a facility showing how you may be connected to one of your targets, indicating who you should contact to seek an introduction. With a subscription, more useful information is available and more specific criteria can be set. Take a look at what is available and decide for yourself if this is an advantage to your prospecting.

You can attempt a similar approach with **Facebook**, and the two together will yield much information as to likely personnel for you to target. Other platforms are available and can be interrogated in a similar fashion.

A specific target can be found by asking a contact on **Twitter.** On this platform, it appears to be acceptable to be blunt: "I'm looking for an introduction to...., could anyone oblige?" I think that's within the character count!

The Benefits of your Own Network of Contacts

Use your network of contacts both live and digitally on LinkedIn and Facebook, to ask if they have any contacts at the targeted company.

If they do, at best you will have an introduction or a referral, at worst you may have the name of someone you can call to ask for the name of the person in the position you are targeting or who can transfer you to the right person. Such referrals prevent any PECR concerns as it bypasses the 'cold-call' approach.

If you can find the name of almost any employee, you can contact them and ask for the name of the intended contact. They are less likely to be expected to 'keep the gate closed' and so will be more willing to pass on this information. They may even transfer the call for you! But, could this be classed as a manipulation....?

As this last suggestion may result in not only finding the right target, but actually being connected on the same call, it is imperative you have something to say that will be effective in grabbing their Attention, developing their Interest, creating the Desire to work with you, as well as giving a call to Action that will help you move toward a sale. (The next section will help with the contacting activity needed once you have identified the most suitable target.)

....and finally, a word of warning

Failing all of these methods for targeting contacts, you still have the option of sub-terfuge or downright deceit. I do not recommend this, not just on ethical grounds, but *you will be found out* and this will, in all certainty, close the door to you for some considerable time!

You have made your lists, and you have identified your ideal contact.
How do you make contact, and what do you say?

Read on....!

CHAPTER 5

MAKING CONTACT

From the first contact, your aim should be to structure and control or lead the sale to achieve a positive and mutually beneficial outcome.

It needs to be mutually beneficial because if the benefits are too one-sided, then the buyer would be less interested in repeating the selling/buying experience with you.

Taking a straw poll of experienced salespeople, I was able to confirm my suspicion, that by far the majority of sales experiences are hampered by **two barriers** put up by salespeople. It has nothing to do with the prospect or the situation and boils down to the self-confidence and 'limiting beliefs' of the salesperson in the following two areas of the sales process which literally 'limits' their success:

Which two areas? CONTACTING and CLOSING!

CONTACTING limiting beliefs develop along these lines:

'They probably think I'm cold calling and want to sell them something...'
Maybe, BUT you have a genuine reason to call, AND you can demonstrate a the likelihood of a 'legitimate interest', and, what do you have to lose?!

'This is a bad time of day; they aren't likely to be in...'
ASSUMPTIONS!

'They are unlikely to want what I have to offer...'
ASSUMPTIONS. How do YOU know this is the case?

'They're going to say 'no' which will damage my confidence/belief...'
ASSUMPTIONS, all most likely to be completely incorrect!

As Robert Louis Stevenson said, 'Everyone lives by selling something'.
Business to consumer (B2C) requires one approach, while business to business (B2B) should, in theory, be more straightforward. Not necessarily easier, but perhaps more easily structured.

Here are some key points in preparation for making contact, B to B:

- Identify and target the decision maker(s), and influencers.
- Research the target company and personnel; the product range and their identified way forward.
- Decide the best method of contact and prepare a strategy for commencing a business relationship.

First, we will start with contacting Business to Consumer:

As a customer or 'consumer', when contacted you are likely to be in familiar surroundings of your own making and choice. Any unwanted contact is likely to be regarded as an invasion of privacy and this is likely to include 'cold-calling'. The introduction of the General Data Protection Regulation and Privacy and Electronic Communication Regulations has helped in this respect but this unwanted 'phone-spamming' is still common, particularly from foreign call centres. Any call from an unknown or withheld number is still regarded with suspicion. If the consumer decides to pick up the 'phone, their response is unlikely to be a jolly 'hello'! The opportunity for a sale is thus reduced to minimal at best. With the GDPR & PECR, much care is needed to avoid becoming a spammer and to ensure contact can be justified and warranted.

How do businesses involved in B-to-C selling overcome these issues? Some with weak justification will still take the cold-calling route and hire teams to work their way through ***very long lists***. Here, economies of scale come into play. If they are converting only one in 500 calls into a sale, that sale value must cover the cost of all 500 calls, plus a significant margin on top, for this strategy to be fully justified. Clearly, this is the case for a lot of businesses; hence the high number of cold calls!

The other, and I believe more effective, socially acceptable and legal strategy, is to use the process outlined in the previous section. In other words, you undertake a comprehensive analysis of a carefully selected group of suspects and turn them into at least warm prospects. Once you have identified those that fully fit your target criteria and have applied your selected filters, so that they are much more likely to be interested in talking to you, you can consider making the first contact, or better still, what marketers call the first 'touch'.

The Marketing 'Touch'

A 'touch' is described as any moment that a prospect has come into contact or experienced something directly related to your company and products:

- *they have seen an advertisement*
- *they have received a flyer*
- *they have come across the company name on social media*
- *they have received an invitation to connect on Linked In*

They say that it takes five to seven touches before a sale becomes possible. By then, the prospect will have achieved an understanding of your company and ethos, your products and services, and the potential benefits of using them. Any contact made once this is achieved will no longer be cold but will stand a very good chance of developing into a sale.

What can you do to manifest these 'touches' and create this 'warm' contact?

Here are some ideas:

1. If you have their names, personalise the contact in any way you can
2. Send them a flyer, with a covering letter, and in that letter...
3. Mention that you will be calling them at a particular time so that any call you make will be expected
4. Offer them a simple opt-out, perhaps in the form of an email response saying simply, 'no-thanks'
5. Do the same as 2-4 above, but by email
6. Send a letter and flyer and follow-up with an email heralding the intended call

Better still....

TIP: If you know their email address from LinkedIn, Facebook or previous contact, use the following strategy to make sure the call is at least a **warm-contact**, and one who won't be surprised or upset to receive your call:

The Salient Contact Warming Strategy (the CWS for short)

1. ***'Seed' the market with your message on appropriate materials.***
2. ***If including the internet, invite a subscription to your newsletter***
3. ***If found on Linked-In or Facebook, invite a connection (personalised)***
4. ***Send out an internet newsletter (include the opt-out option)***
5. ***Note who opens the email, and...***

6. ***Send them a personal letter and/or email suggesting the call, again with the opt-out***
7. ***If they are still there after this, they have a genuine interest, so...CALL THEM!***

(This works with B2B as well as B2C.)

This is a great way to be sure of a good reception. You have made a good impression and provided sufficient background knowledge of you and your company to help ensure the prospect will answer favourably. In this way, you have achieved **Prospect Buy-In**: developed some interest, even some desire to find out more, and suggested the call-to-action; to answer your call.

Which would you prefer to do? Call hundreds of numbers, receive nearly as many negative responses for a 1 in 500 chance of a sale, *or*, do some basic investigation of your suspects and follow a simple but thorough contacting strategy to achieve a **warm-contact** and the best chance of making a sale? Point made; I think!

Business to Business:

Having read the B2C approach above, you will likely have realised that B2B need not be much different. The most significant difference will be that any cold calling made to larger businesses is even less likely to be tolerated and will be intercepted before it reaches any decision makers or their influencers.

The Contact Warming Strategy described above will be required in most cases and will be just as effective.

The point is, for a sale to be made efficiently, effectively and with the least resistance, you need to have built some credibility and become an attractive proposition to any prospect you are wanting to contact.

If you have:

- devised an attractive and effective message
- done your homework and are sure that the target will find your offer an advantage and suitable to fit their needs
- 'seeded' the market with appropriate promotional material
- followed the Contact Warming Strategy, and then...
- CALLED THEM – or made some form of direct contact, with the opt-out

...then you stand the best chance of receiving a positive and encouraging reception with the best chance of a sale.

Having given yourself the best chance of a good reception, you pick up the telephone.

What should you say?

NOW we have reached the tricky bit for a lot of people. If you have prepared as described above, you should have few worries about your reception. Yet, that barrier of lifting the telephone can still cause some anxiety in even the thickest-skinned salespeople!

The larger the company, more decision makers and influencers there are likely to be, and often from different backgrounds. They could be purchasing management or personnel, but they could just as easily be a technical manager, chief engineer, or senior specialist. In these cases, your key words will need to change. To illustrate this point:

(As well as showing you can fulfil the primary need).

- An MD or FD is interested in cost and profit (known as the 'economic buyer'): focus on being *"Cost-effective"* and showing the good *"return on investment"*
- A Technical, Ops, or Specialist is interested in benefits, features ('user buyer'): use words such as *"Faster, flexible and feature-packed"*
- A Purchaser interested in price, delivery, supplier status, ('commercial buyer'): impress them with *"high value, competitive, fast-turn-round, and respected"*

In short, identify and target their greatest interest or motivation.

The following are ideas that are tried, tested, proven and used. I acknowledge every situation is different and their responses can still catch you out but having something ready as a 'way-in' is useful and advised. If your target is a small company, then you are more likely to be put straight through. The larger the company, the more difficult it can be to gain direct access. The following covers some tips and techniques for improving your chances of access:

Scenario 1

If you have used the Contact Warming Strategy (CWS) above, then you can ask for the person you have identified and contacted by email or letter because:

"they are expecting my call"

Bingo you're through! That was easy wasn't it!

Sorry, yes, this is real life and there will be times when it just doesn't work or doesn't fit the response you have received. Here are some more ideas....

Scenario 2

You have a genuine recommendation or referral from someone you know is connected with your target.

"I have been asked by (your contact) to call 'x' in relation to....",

The credibility of your connection will help to persuade the gatekeeper to connect you: ***"(Your contact) suggested I call as he believes it could be of mutual benefit".***

Scenario 3

Perhaps you cannot find the name of the specific contact but are determined to get through. Simply ask. If necessary, explain more of the reason why. Be prepared to do this as succinctly and professionally as possible; you will not make progress if you waffle vaguely about the subject of the call. If you have a sentence or two ready that describes the potential advantages of working with you and using your products, they will react more favourably.

Using the *CWS* above will make calling easier, but if that wasn't possible, it would be a good time to introduce our favourite character in every company; our friend....

There are many ways of engaging and interacting with gatekeepers. Handled wrongly they can close the door on you for good. Handled well they can become your friend and subsequently OPEN DOORS for you.

Who are the Gatekeepers?

Gate-Keepers - Part 1

Over the years, I have found that the 'Gate-Keepers' have become more tenacious! Gatekeepers can be the tightly controlled receptionist or the PA of the target. Either of these roles can block what you may consider to be a polite and justified contact.

At one extreme, you have the companies who refuse to give out the names of their employees even if you request speaking to someone with a specific job title. This is very frustrating when you are looking to have a professional discussion to establish a need for your products.

At the other extreme, you have gate-keepers who will tell you the name of your ideal target but will refuse to put you through unless and until you have explained the full reason for the call and then say that the contact is very busy and likely to be so for the next seventeen years. (I may have exaggerated to make the point.)

Unfortunately, in my view, this whole situation has been brought about by the dreaded untrained and unguided 'cold callers' (yes, it's them again); those who have a very long list of 'suspects' and will call on the off-chance simply to meet a call rate that is flashing on their office wall. The result is that hard-working professionals are interrupted and disturbed to answer some trite questions, often from a script, and usually totally unrelated to the work or interest of those targeted. It's hardly surprising that the gatekeepers have become more protective making business-to-business conversations much more difficult to arrange and limiting of the cross-fertilisation of ideas, stifling innovation and invention.

(I may have mentioned before that cold-calling has its place in some markets, but in the vast majority of cases you should use Salient techniques to turn these cold calls into hot-contacts, as described above.) Back to the gatekeepers:

Gate-Keepers - Part 2

Gatekeepers are just doing their jobs! Some are helpful and flexible; others are authoritarian and obstructive. Their real job title could be Receptionist, PA, Deputy...., Assistant to the......., Office Manager, or Secretary.

Whatever, their title, when it comes to receiving telephone calls, they have but two fears:

1. *Putting through the wrong call*
2. *Blocking the one they should have put through*

They may have strict instructions as to who to put through, or the type of call to block. On the other hand, they may have discretion in who they can let through.

Whatever they are called, whatever they have been told, you need to get through to the decision maker. What can you do to make this more likely?

What kind of approach will NOT work with a gatekeeper?
Grovelling / Sycophancy / Pulling rank / Instructing / Obvious manipulation

I say 'OBVIOUS manipulation' because clever and discreet manipulation could work, but then is it right anyway? Plus, there's always the chance that you could be found out, resulting in their closing the door for good and damaging your own reputation.

An extreme example involved a saleswoman who asked to be put through to a prospect claiming to be his wife! The secretary announced her as 'someone who says she's your wife'. When the saleswoman was firmly put in her place by the prospect, she protested that the secretary had mis-heard or misunderstood- a second lie that caused the prospect to contact the MD of the firm she represented. The MD was shocked and apologetic. When quizzed, the lady could not at first see what was wrong. It turned out she had been trained in high pressure telesales and was applying what to her was common practice. Needless to say, she was 're-trained'.

Gate-Keepers - Part 3

A simple code of conduct for dealing with gatekeepers:

- Treat them with respect – they have a job to do and they want to do their best for the company and their boss.
- Treat them like a million-pound customer- you value the opportunity to engage with them.
- Be honest and open- they are not stupid and spend more time fielding such calls as you do in making them.
- If frosty, apologise for interrupting their day- ***'have I called at a bad time?'***

• Show humility; include gentle humour if appropriate; try and 'win-them-over' (but again, don't fawn or falsely flatter.)
• Do not leave a message as these are open to interpretation and misunderstandings.
• State your company position. If you do not yet have seniority, state you are calling on behalf of the MD or SD, but clear that with them first!

In my early career I developed many successful methods of contacting decision methods. Some were not fully ethical even then. It would be wrong of me to explain and elaborate them here. However, having met the 'Telephone Assassin' I saw value in some of his approaches when dealing with gatekeepers. His ideas are excellent for overcoming some of the gatekeeping tactics which are designed to prevent you making contact with the decision makers. My favourite of his many tactics are:

If you cannot find their name but want to target an individual in a specific role; call to check their address and post code and ask:
"who should I make it specifically 'for the attention of...?"

If they ask you to 'send details';
"I'd love to send you something, but I won't know what to send until I have spoken to...
'If I sent general information, I'd be spamming. When should I call them?"

If they ask you what it's about, say:
"It's important but not urgent, when should I call back?"
Do not give the gatekeeper the opportunity to decline your offer and close the gate.

If they offer to ask your target person to call you back:
"I'd love to take their call, but I'm busy too and I'm keen to avoid 'telephone-tennis' so when would be the best time to call back?"

These suggestions are courtesy of the 'Telephone Assassin', Mr. Anthony Stears. He offers a clever and dynamic way with telephone techniques. www.anthonystears.co.uk
NB. Please remember that most gatekeepers are not fools and are likely to spot such 'tricks-of-the-trade', even benign ones described above. Always make friends first and ask for their help.

The Salient Targeted Contacting System takes you through a simple logical process that should make the activity more straightforward, easily applied and, dare I say, more enjoyable?! See what you think:

The Salient
CONTACT WARMING SYSTEM

- **Market Research** – learn as much as you can about the market and the relationship of your target company/person has to that market.

- **Website Study** – find out their strengths and potential weaknesses; their present projects and product/service offerings and their forward thinking.

- **LinkedIn and/or Facebook** – use to identify specific targets – position, name and anything else you can find out. Request a contact (personalise).

- **Mutual Connections** – once identified, and using the same resources, see if there are any mutual connections that you could use to ask for an introduction, and/or a referral.

- **Other Employee** – if you have a target role but cannot identify a specific name, either call and ask using the processes above to identify another employee and contact them or use one of the phrases listed above. (Questionable ethically)

- **Gatekeeper Confrontation** – if you are come up against by a Gatekeeper, remember the following simple rules:
  - Make friends, they can be a very valuable ally.
  - Gain credibility by talking with confidence and authority.
  - And, only as a last resort, call before 9 or after 5!

(A boss will likely work before and/or after these times, whereas a gatekeeper less so. Only use this as a last resort; if they find they have been by-passed, they may become obstructive in subsequent contacts. Again, ethically questionable)

Tip: *When dealing with gatekeepers simply* ***ask for their help****. While they are not there to fulfil your need, they may find it difficult to refuse to help.*

All the above has been about how to identify and target a specific person, hopefully the decision maker, who will appreciate the advantage and benefits of purchasing your products and/or services. Always refer to the requirements of GDPR & PECR to be sure of your ground.

What to say when you are put through to your Target

- This is the first chance you have to build a positive relationship.
- Mistakes made now are very difficult to put right.
- Ask questions and LISTEN CAREFULLY to the responses.
- Keep listening while you make your case and move towards achieving the objective of the call: to **arrange to talk again, or better still, to meet to discuss possibilities.**

First words are very important - First impressions are critical.

FIRST RULES:

1. **Have a clear objective**
2. **Identify a named target or contact, or at least a title**
3. **Identify an alternative contact and be ready to speak with them**
4. **Decide your opening line**
5. **Speak clearly, stick to the point and do not rush**
6. **Speak with confidence and authority**
7. **Do not assume familiarity unless invited**
8. **Apply AIDA (attention, interest, desire, action) referring to your selected 'message'**
9. **State the reason for the call, i.e. what you understand is their need, target the need, and start to fulfil the need**
10. **Work out some 'what ifs'**
11. **Have a clear call-to-action**
12. **Have a fall-back plan (sending details, subscribe to your newsletter, request alternative contact, call at a future date if timing wrong, etc.)**
13. **Thank, summarise, clarify and confirm the conversation by email**
14. **Complete any agreed follow-up**

SOME SUGGESTED CALL OBJECTIVES - in priority order

1. To obtain an order, or at least arrange a further meeting
2. To arrange a video call, or to extend the call, in order to develop further interest
3. To arrange to call again, when more time is available
4. To agree to exchange emails providing more background detail – again developing interest
5. For them to accept some form of regular contact – a newsletter or blog
6. To obtain a definite 'no thanks', to be able to move onto the next prospect

The words and phrases you use can depend on many aspects of the business relationship you can and need to foster. It can depend on –

- Yours and their seniority
- The contact's tone of voice
- Whether they are targeted by you, or have simply picked up the call
- Your chosen call objectives
- The way the contact responds to your first comments and introduction

POSSIBLE OPENING LINES: ***(following introductions)***

Refer to your mutual connection to gain credibility, then:

> ***"I saw on your website...."***
> ***"I believe you use/are developing/are active in the area of...."***
> ***"Have you considered the benefits available from....?"***
> ***"Is there a conversation to be had around this issue?"***

Once dialogue is commenced, aim to establish the need. Then, target the need using....

STEERING LINES:

> ***"Could our approach provide the solution/benefits you need?"***
> ***"So, if we could provide that solution...."***
> ***"Would it be an advantage to you if you/we could...."***

Use the "if...then...and, therefore" approach to show how you can fulfil the need ...and then move to an interim close; summarize, agree to meet and to move matters forward. (An 'interim close' is where you aim for agreement up to a particular point. This helps both parties focus on the close and can make it more difficult for the buyer to return to your competition).

CLOSING LINES:

> ***"Rather than discuss details over the 'phone, can we meet to confirm what we've discussed and perhaps move this forward?"***
> ***"I have some more information/ideas I'd like to share with you. Shall we get together to look at them more thoroughly...?"***
> ***"I'd be happy to give you and your colleagues/team a presentation..."***
> ***"....... when would be a good time to meet up?"***

It is at a subsequent meeting that a full presentation or 'pitch' will be required.

ALWAYS follow-up by email with a summary of the conversation and the actions agreed, even if it is only to keep them on your contact list.

And finally, I am often asked; *"what if they are consistently unavailable,* how often and how many times should I try?"
It depends on how helpful or optimistic the expectation of the contact. If they sound keen, try 3, perhaps 4 times. If disinterested I would try no more than 2 or 3 times. At that point, either send details and try again in a few weeks with a 'warmer' contact (one you have called before), or try another route completely, or even another contact within the company.

No contact system is fool-proof and every target and contact scenario is different. This system, and the previous planning and prospecting sections, should provide enough ideas for you to plan your approaches with alternative routes to your target to give you a good chance of success. The more options you can identify, the more likely you are of contacting the right person to open up your opportunity for a sale.

THE SALIENT POINTS

1. Don't assume anything – ASK
2. Research the market, the target, everything you can
3. Prepare – your objectives, and your key phrases for opening, steering and closing
4. Identify your primary, and a secondary contact
5. Seed the market, then follow the Salient Contact Warming System
6. Contact them, by now they should be expecting it!
7. Close by agreeing a way forward

Make sure every contact is a good contact.

In the following section, we have reached the stage when the target has been identified and contacted and a meeting agreed. The opportunity and the need has been identified and at least part clarified. Further discussion is required to complete the understanding of the need on one side and the offer on the other. This is commenced (and sometimes completed) at the first meeting; *the meeting where the first (and sometimes last) pitch or presentation is made.*

CHAPTER 6:

PITCHING AND PRESENTATIONS

The difference between a pitch and a presentation:
If what you are presenting is anything directly aimed at achieving a sale, then it is also a pitch. Be it one-to-one sitting at a table or assisted by various media and standing in front of an audience, you are presenting your case AND making your pitch.

If the intention is to 'make a case' for something, to inform, or to demonstrate, then this becomes more of a presentation. This too can be achieved on a small or large scale. This should follow the same rules as the pitch, and steer/show the audience the benefits of considering a proposition that will be favourable.

A good salesperson will switch seamlessly between the two as needed.

There can be much variation in how your company, the product, and your offer is pitched or presented. This depends on a number of criteria:

- The type of product
- The value of the product
- The value of the business opportunity
- The importance of the opportunity
- The level & type of anticipated competition
- The size of the target company, and sometimes,
- The seniority of the target decision maker

To add a little detail:
The type of product – if it's more of a 'commodity' such as printing ink, or website design, then a short pitch may be sufficient.
The value of the product – if each device or service package is worth a considerable amount of money, then a well-produced presentation may be required, and often to a number of key staff.
The value of the business opportunity – regardless of the single unit cost, if the business is substantial in value, then a full presentation is likely to be expected.
The importance of the opportunity – if the target company is of strategic benefit to you, perhaps in opening doors to other opportunities or benefits, then it would be worthwhile increasing the status and professionalism of the pitch/presentation.
The size of the target company – from my experience, as a rule of thumb, the larger the company, the more impressive the presentation required. Yet I have, at the customer's

request and on a number of occasions, given a makeshift presentation to a rapidly convened board meeting of a relatively small company, and won the business!

The seniority of the target person – Managing Directors of larger companies have high expectations. Often, they will expect salespeople to have to work hard to win the deal and so need to be pampered with the most professional of presentations; sometimes with a team, sometimes to just themselves.

A good mix of prior research and managing expectations when making arrangements with your primary contact will help to clarify how you will need to be prepared. Always over-prepare to prevent awkward surprises!

How you present yourself, your company and your products depends on the individual circumstances of the meeting. For example, the structure and focus of the presentation will differ if you have met before; if they know of your company, if they are an existing customer, or if their business is technical, specialist or commercially focused. The presentation could be requested, needed, or offered for a number of reasons:

- **To provide company background and credibility**
- **To describe products or services and introduce case studies**
- **As part of the sales process to help present and/or close the business**
- **To inform and educate about a specific topic or expertise within your remit**

If you really want to impress, always aim to exceed expectations. The simple way of achieving this is to present your case at a professional level a little higher than expected in the situation.

The following are some ideas you may like to follow:

- If they are expecting to be handed leaflets, produce a comprehensive brochure
- If they are expecting a free pen, give them a free sample
- If they expect to be talked-to while being shown flyers, show them a laptop presentation as well
- If they are expecting a simple slide presentation, include a video and a case study
- If you hear they are rolling out one of the senior decision makers, take along someone of similar level of experience or expertise
- Mix and match all the above as appropriate and available

If you are unsure of what they are expecting, ***ask them!*** Try not to fall into the trap of structuring a presentation to match the request for 'oh, just something simple'. Too often, they will subsequently invite the MD. For this reason, it is a good idea to check who is attending and confirm the day before. Do not be caught out. Have a contingency of something a bit better than was anticipated.

Pitching or presenting in this way will demonstrate many positive attributes. You will be seen as keen, professional, astute, focused and 'on-the-ball'. You will make a good impression and start to build profitable relationships.

Essential preparation – it is important to:

Define Objectives

As with all such activities, the first action must be to define objectives for the pitch or presentation. What do you want to achieve, what do they want to achieve? What are their needs and expectations and what call-to-action do you wish to achieve at the end of it?

Manage Expectations

Agree the type of presentation expected and the topic and scope of the content. It could include also a call to action or a 'close' relevant to the stage reached in the sales process.

Structure with AIDA (Attention, Interest, Desire, Action)

Ultimately, your aim is not to sell to them, but to help them to decide to buy from you. This is an important distinction. A presentation that has a clear structure with helpful facts and figures and addresses their specific needs, will be better received than a blatant sales pitch focusing on the wonderful things your company does. It should still follow, with a call to action at the end, but the aim should not be to sell, but to increase your credibility, develop their interest and desire to work with you.

Target the Need

A full knowledge and understanding of the customers' needs is essential to ensure it is relevant and achieves the objectives. Unless it is an introductory presentation showing the whole company, then it is important to have fully identified and qualified the need before structuring your 'pitch'.

Be Prepared

If you supply to a range of business sizes, then it would be an advantage to have more than one level of presentation. An adaptable, small presentation would suit most SMEs, whereas a larger, more expensive looking approach is often expected by larger companies.

Key Points to include in a Pitch or a Presentation

- In both cases, remember you are building a relationship with the buyer(s) or interested parties. You are not selling to them; you are making a good case to help them *buy from you.*
- Smile and make regular eye-contact (not constant – this can be unnerving).
- Keep asking questions to fully qualify their needs and confirm their 'buy-in'.
- Target that need in a clear and positive way.
- Tell a story or present a short case study that is at least close to their particular need and application.
- Demonstrate the value of working with you; quote testimonials where relevant.
- *Summarise your presentation, focusing on fulfilling their needs and your objectives.*

A Simple Structure for a Pitch

This assumes that the full professional preamble is complete, including introductions and a series of questions required to identify and clarify that the need is at least underway. An initial pitch can then be attempted.

The ***'if, then and therefore'*** questioning approach.

"IF your need is ....,
THEN you are looking for someone to provide a solution along the lines of.......,
THEREFORE, if we can fulfil this need and more, would you be happy to consider us as a supplier?" ......or words to that effect. After that, the detail is agreed, negotiated and the deal closed. This approach sets up and manages expectations and gives you the initial buy-in to help smooth the way forward for a sale. (Details of the rest of the sales process are found in the following chapters.)

Caution: Focusing on a specific need at the outset may be wasting time if the prospect is only trying to determine your suitability as a supplier! Likewise, don't talk about your and your company's background and credentials when your prospect is ready to talk in detail of their specific need. Here we are back to my war cry of "ASK THEM!"

'Would you like to hear about our company and how we could become an effective supplier to you?'

They are likely to have studied your website first otherwise this meeting would not be taking place, so do not make this an epic of Wagnerian proportions! 5-10 minutes for the history will almost certainly be plenty, depending on the type and size of meeting and the age and size of your own company. Follow this with another 5 minutes or so describing your present capability and finally bring in a few case studies, even testimonials of companies who have been privileged to work with you in the past! Try and finish on a note relevant to the need they have and bring it back to your hope to be able to supply against that need.

'I hope that shows how we have developed the expertise and resources to become an experienced/major/effective supplier to you of ....

As a first pitch and to fill in any missing background that will help to increase your credibility and chances as a supplier, the following is a broad summary. This will achieve the buy-in you will need to be able to develop the discussion and the relationship and to present, negotiate and agree the detail of the deal.

1. ***Ask about their company and their role within the company***
2. ***Ask about the need they have that brought you to this meeting***
3. ***Clarify that need to manage expectations and help steer your pitch***
4. ***Ask if they would like to hear a little company background and show how you could become their supplier of choice for that need***
5. ***Build credibility with company history, past experiences, vision & mission****
6. ***Demonstrate how you would approach their problem/need***
7. ***Increase your credibility and their confidence by introducing case studies and/or testimonials***
8. ***Keep checking you are including as many DMs (Decision Makers) and influencers as possible***
9. ***Either continue then to cover all details, negotiate and close, or, arrange to meet again to cover the full requirements of the deal***

The structure and length of such a pitch depends on many aspects: the complexity of the need and/or your products; the size and value of the business opportunity; the seniority and number of the decision makers and their influencers seeking to be convinced.

A good salesperson will adapt to all these variables, be fully prepared, and rise to the occasion!

A Simple Structure for a Presentation

As suggested above, a presentation may be required instead of a pitch. This may be because the prospect feels that it is more time effective to gather all the DMs, influencers and/or 'stakeholders' together to experience the same presentation.

A presentation is more of a performance and moves firmly into the realms of the dreaded 'public speaking'! They say that after dying and divorce, public speaking is the most stressful activity for anyone who attempts it. Maybe, but only for those who are less than fully prepared.

As with all sales activities, PREPARATION is key.

- **Define the need clearly**
- **Define your objectives fully**
- **Have the full presentation structure designed**
- **Ensure it covers all aspects of the need**
- **Follow AIDA, describing the advantage and benefits**
  - **Develop credibility and commitment as you progress**
  - **End on a call to action: e.g. to move this forward together**
- **Target the need**
- **Focus on the positives and the value you can add to their business**
- **Ensure you have answers for all likely questions**
- **Have contingencies for all unlikely questions and occurrences**
- **Return to the big advantage and your commitment to them**

Once the above is clear and defined, a 'script' in the form of bulleted points or a 'mind-map' can be constructed. I would try and avoid a fully scripted speech as this will diminish the impact and engagement of a good presentation. Have key words or lines to hand, so as to avoid loss of position or focus, but ***do not read a script!***

With the above fully defined, then confidence should be high for this presentation as it 'covers all bases'. But what do we say, and in particular, how do we start?

There are many options for this, but most presentations I have attended will start with ***'Hello my name is... and I'm from ... Today I am going to tell you about... etc.'***

Every time I hear this first sentence from a presenter my heart sinks. I know that from then on, it is likely to be the driest and most tedious presentation since the last dry and tedious presentation I heard- and I have heard a good many!

I had developed my own structure that improved on this mind-numbing style, but I am indebted to my friend Michael Trigg - the 'Presentation Maestro'* (www.presentationmaestro.com) f**or showing me a simple, superior approach. It adds key points that are engaging and memorable and are totally applicable in a variety of situations. Put as simply as possible, the process involves:**

Greeting:

- A simple thank you to the introducer
- A greeting to all present; 'good morning' or as appropriate
- Acknowledgement of any key attendees (if politic to do so).

Topic:

- Introduce the big issue grabbing their attention and referencing their need:
- ***'You will have noticed that...'***
- ***'According to... the trend in this market is to...***
- ***Many companies are not in any position or state to address this potentially huge problem. Those that are not prepared, could risk their survival.'***

Introduction:

- State or restate your name
- Give your credentials succinctly- why you are qualified and sufficiently knowledgeable and experienced to provide advice, guidance, and solutions:
- ***'I am... of... and have been working in this sector with specific responsibility for...***
- ***I have considerable experience and insight into this issue having provided solutions for a number of the key operators including... and ...***

No further elaboration is necessary, as they are likely to have 'looked you up' before you arrived and/or will quiz you in detail if they feel they need more background.

Aim:

- State just ONE aim to make significant positive change that will go some way, or maybe completely solve their problem or fulfil their need:
- ***'In the next.... minutes, I will demonstrate how we can help you to address this issue, provide a workable solution that fits your company needs and overcome any of the negative aspects that can be associated with the problem'.***

Agenda:

- Announce that the presentation will be in three parts:
    1. **Clarifying the issue** emphasising how it relates to the company.
    2. **Outlining the risks** of the issue and the negative effects of inaction.
    3. **Offering the solution** as to how your proposal will make the difference, they seek for the situation to remain or become positive and to be an advantage to their company.

- Once announced, 'signpost' the section of the agenda at each stage to help attendees keep track of the logical structure and to anticipate the good things to come from the solution you offer!
    1. ***'First we look at the issues in more detail...'***
    2. ***'Now we have a full understanding of the issues, let's take a look at the effects, risks and likely problems caused by these issues...'***
    3. ***'Knowing what issues we face and the likely effects, risks and problems arising from them, at..., we have a solution that should at least miti gate these issues, if not fully overcome their potential negative impact. What we offer is a solution whereby....'***

Having Completed the three sections, we move to the...

Summary:-

- A short précis of the points in the agenda and/or
- A short confirmation that the stated Aim has been achieved.
- ***'With this solution ... (their company) ...will overcome any or all such issues deriving from the problem highlighted at the start' or***
- ***appropriate words to that effect.***

And finally, the Call-To-Action:

Next Step (Action):

- A call-to-action is essential to maintaining engagement and the potential to supply the solution.
- ***Refer back to the advantage of using you, your company and your solution and challenge them to make the change that you propose.***

That, in brief, is a presentation structure, but what about the audience response?

Questions:

- A simple technique when handling **questions** is to repeat it back to the questioner to be sure you have understood it, which also gives you time to gather your thoughts and arrive at a starting point for the answer.

Objections:

Objections are a different issue. Your response will depend on the issue raised:

Questioning the relevance:

- Offer the logic you used to include it in your presentation or,
- Offer it as interesting background- potentially useful if matters were to move in a particular direction (only if you can identify this possible direction!)

Questioning the effectiveness

- Refer to case studies.
- Offer testimonials where similar difficulties were overcome.
- Explain that you have applied significant time, effort and experience to the issue and that analysis of the options, risks, ramifications and all potential strategies have led you to believe in your optimum solution.

Questioning your credibility or suitability to apply yourselves to this task:

- Offer chapter and verse outlining your team's experience, level of qualifications, intense commitment and dedication.
- the testimonials of multiple happy customers!

After the presentation ideally you need to remain in control, at least until your defined objective is achieved, that is, to move towards commitment to the sale.

- An open approach to this would involve the question:
  'We hope this has addressed your thoughts and concerns about your needs in full. Are we now in a position to move forward with this?
- A negative response simply begs the follow-up question:
  'What can we do to help to move this forward'.

It is very likely they will tell you, so do it and move on!

Having prospected, identified, contacted and presented and pitched to our prospective customers, we ask ourselves the question, 'Are they still interested?' Of course they are, because you have been nothing less than impressive!
However, you can always check by undertaking an

Interim close' which simply involves asking the question:

- ***'Do you believe this will fulfil your need/solve the problem/provide the solution you need?'***

Because of your professional approach to the sale and the considerable preparation and thoroughness you have achieved, the answer will be either 'Yes', or 'Nearly'. Either way, we can then move to the next stage in the process; the sales activity known as '**Negotiation'.**

In the unlikely event that the answer is 'no', it is likely to be due to their not sharing all the relevant information with you. Two simple questions should help:

- ***'What have we missed?'***
- ***'What can we do to put this back on track?'***

Offer a short summary of how you see the issue and ask for theirs to see where they might differ.

Finally remember the Salient points mentioned earlier whereby:

- Technical or Specialist personnel have different needs and priorities to those of the commercial team. They will each respond to different approaches, strategies and words.
- If the presentation is of a more broad approach, try and ensure that all DMs and influencers from technical/specialist and commercial teams are attending. If not, offer to make two separate and differently structured presentations.
- As with all contacting situations, whenever any issue is discussed, presented or agreed: **Summarise, Clarify and Confirm these points to every person involved.**
- Have a distinct call to action and agree it as the way forward for both parties

Pitching and presenting can be fun and very rewarding. Using a simple process of preparation and a structure that is easy to apply and operate, the potential stress of this activity will be reduced to more comfortable levels.

An unstressed presenter will be able to engage better with the contact or attendees and will be more successful at imparting the information and generating understanding.

An engaged and understanding audience are far more likely to respond positively to your call-to-action.

A good pitch or presentation will ensure good progress to achieving the sale and building lasting business relationships.

Presenting and Pitching for the sale are both very important parts of the sales process. With sufficient preparation and careful structure, it can be relatively stress free and even enjoyable! Done well, it will result in prospects and targets being influenced positively and a likely favourable outcome. It should make any negotiation that now follows, that much easier.

CHAPTER 7:

NEGOTIATION

IF (and it is a big if) the prospects like your product or service; are happy with all the customer support offered; the level of quality; your credibility and the company's credibility; the price; the delivery and the colour; in short, it's exactly what they want, then they should not need to negotiate. They will just pay you the money and be grateful.

How often does that happen? In the real world, from my experience, almost never. There is always something that needs to be negotiated.

OK, so commodity retail selling is an exception to this. Few people dare to arrive at the till and start to attempt to negotiate the price!

I confess, I enjoy negotiation. It gives you the chance to engage with the prospect on another level, often requiring much thinking-on-the-feet and allowing some creativity. However, it can also be a bit of a minefield: an over-eager comment can dramatically reduce your chances of achieving a good deal; missing some key comment or clue from the buyer can prevent the best deal from being achieved.

In short, saying or doing the wrong thing can prevent you from winning the sale!

This stage of the process can bring out the true colours of your contact or the 'buyer'. It is not uncommon for an amiable, amenable, easy-going buyer to turn into a hard-nosed, bargain-focused negotiator at this point. Beware! They may be hiding a qualification from the Attila-the-Hun School for Hardened Buyers. Many negotiations could then become very confrontational with each side trying to score points off the other.

With pressure placed on every salesperson to win deals, various clever, but highly manipulative, techniques were developed, and sadly, some are still used today.
Yet with over 20 years plus of field sales and management, I proved time and again that a good customer relationship builds a customer base of supporters who will be pleased to do more and more business with you.

The Dark Side of Negotiation

I bought a book in 1999. Actually, I bought a few, but this one was relevant to the topic: 'Negotiating Skills' by Tim Hindle and published by Dorling Kindersley. It has caused me, and many of those attending my courses much amusement. There is a chapter called 'Weakening the other party's Position'. Within it is a table outlining the tactics you can use to weaken the opposition.

In this table are five headings. The first is Financial and this explains how you can 'inform' and 'point out' various aspects that need to be considered. This all reads well. Then we get to the fun parts. Under 'Legal' the author suggests you 'threaten to pursue a course of legal action', emphasising the cost of lengthy legal wrangles in terms of time and money.

Moving on to the 'Social' section, it says to 'tell your opponents that their proposals are an insult to the people they are likely to affect'.

Then comes the section called 'Humiliation', in which the instruction is to 'humiliate an opposing party in order to damage their image or reputation', as 'this can cause some long-term damage to their credibility'.

Finally, the section called 'Emotional' encourages you to 'emotionally blackmail your opponent if they are not giving you enough ground'.

In my opinion, this is very unethical selling and it epitomizes the confrontational approach to selling that is still too prevalent. I cannot believe that an 'opponent' (sic) treated in this way will be keen to make concessions in your negotiation and I am very doubtful they would consider repeating the process with you for another business opportunity. Would you go back for more 'humiliation' or 'emotional blackmail'?
No, neither would I. It is exactly this type of approach that moved me to champion Ethical Selling.

Case Study:
I delivered a Technical Sales Course recently, to a team from Samsung in Germany. One of the team had had a difficult experience with a buyer and asked me a difficult question: Where does an ethical salesperson 'draw the line'?

The answer should be simple, and quite straight forward: 'wherever your conscience lets you draw the line'. This is obvious, clear and fits all. However, is it a helpful answer?

The example given by the team member was of a potential customer who used their own 'pressure buying' techniques that quickly strayed into bullying; the Genghis Kahn school of negotiation. Apparently, the buyer would throw his pen onto the table and demand loudly that they accept his terms or get out. Other tactics of similar aggressive and intimidating nature were used. Unfortunately, while he was an experienced sales person, he was not able to walk out on the negotiations as he had been instructed to pursue the business and to win it. Would YOU sit there and take that abuse?

He had my sympathy. Most experienced sales people have had situations of similar severe discomfort. While the buyer rants, raves and threatens, you are sat there wrestling with your own conscience and professionalism. What are your options?

There are many. I offer three:

1/ Fight back? This is the most satisfying. Potentially it can gain respect from the buyer and a mutually beneficial solution could be possible. However, it is extremely risky, as it may escalate the emotions and temper to the point where errors are made, opportunities are lost, and things are said that should never be said by true professionals. Are you reducing your own standards by lowering yourself to their position?

2/ 'Take it on the chin'; in other words, sit there and use silence or passive resistance as your main tool of defense. This is a very professional approach that will make the buyers behavior seem very childish and clearly bullying in comparison. However, there is also the risk that they will then take your reluctance to engage in a fight as weakness and assume their argument has been won.

3/ A carefully judged balance between the two, whereby you respond to aggressive posturing with a firm insistence and repeated 'no'. Your volume would be higher than usual but less than theirs; maintain eye-contact as much as possible; your words would again be professional, but your manner should show you standing firm but being fair. Consistency, professionalism, repetition and firmness are needed, with a clear message that you will not be intimidated.

The salesman was strong and held his ground as best he could. Give-in to a bully and they will always bully you. If you cannot work with them, and you have the authority, you can walk away, but do not let them win.

Yes, it is up to you and your conscience; but do not give in to intimidation. When you can, retain the moral 'high ground' and give little away. No-one likes a bully, and it is a great shame that some believe this is the way to behave in modern society. However, one cannot deny that they still exist, and we must deal with them while achieving our objectives AND remaining professional.

NEGOTIATION

Ideally, this and the following chapter on 'Closing' should be read together.

If you have succeeded in building a good relationship so far, then the rest of the sales process may well continue as smoothly. It may not but all you can do is apply good skills and techniques and prepare to negotiate.

As with all things Salient:

- ***do not assume the smooth process achieved so far will necessarily continue***
- ***be as prepared as possible***
- ***have contingencies or back-up plans***

No two sales follow exactly the same course or pattern. The Salient process is a guide, a template which must at all times be flexible and adaptable. However, as in all stages of the process, preparation, anticipation and some key skills and techniques will assist greatly in achieving the best deal and give you confidence to follow and stick to your objectives.

NB In a large company, teams of negotiators are the norm with members representing the different departments involved or specified roles within the team. The make-up of the team and techniques used by them can be very different from those needed with 'one-to-one, or two' negotiation.

The Salient 'Ultimate Transaction'

In the last few years I have developed what I call the 'Ultimate Transaction'. This is a grand title for a simple system that follows the sales right through from the start of negotiation, through to the final close. It used to be called the 'Salient Ultimate Close' but I changed this when I realised the value of combining the negotiation and closing activities into one simple, but highly effective process.

When negotiating it is important to remain focused on the close, and, an effective close needs to follow effective negotiation.

First, it is important to understand fully the skills and techniques that can make negotiation a very rewarding activity. **But what is negotiation?**

A process involving two or more parties where goods and/or services are exchanged, usually for money. All parties aim to achieve the best deal for themselves and use negotiation as the process with which to reach their objectives.

The reason why we need to negotiate is the disparity between what we offer and what is needed or wanted by the prospective customer. The essence of negotiation is that:

- YOU WANT THE BEST DEAL FOR YOU AND YOUR COMPANY.

- THEY WANT THE BEST DEAL FOR THEIR COMPANY.

The mistake made by most is the assumption that these are mutually exclusive: what is best for your company is not the best for theirs and vice-versa. This assumption makes for a confrontational sale based on a win-lose scenario.

With the Salient approach to negotiation, as long as the deal is made, and they are happy with the deal, then it is a win-win deal and they will be keen to come back for more. At worst you will have had to stretch your bargaining limits by a small, anticipated amount. Ideally, you will have used your skill and experience (and the techniques and ideas explained in this chapter) so that any compromise is within limits and has been well controlled and led by you during the negotiation.

Preparation, careful anticipation and key questions will ensure success.

PREPARATION

When should negotiation start?

The Salient sales process, and the story so far suggests that negotiation commences once the pitch or presentation has been made. Yet, as early as first contact negotiations can be underway - ***'If we can demonstrate our ability to supply this in the type of package you need, then would you be interested in hearing more?'***

If the prospect is keen to purchase your product or services but is hampered by tight budgets or poor cash-flow and if you are still keen to sell to them under these conditions, price negotiation may commence at first contact. But, prior to meeting with them to qualify the need, you may want to ask them ***'What budget have you allocated for this?'*** Such a direct question is valuable to both sides, particularly if the prospect has little idea of the value you provide. If there is a large disparity between their budget and your pricing, it can save a great deal of time and effort identifying this at an early stage. Again, we are managing expectations and avoiding costly assumptions.

What do we need to clarify prior to negotiation?

Before we attempt to make a list of all the aspects or criteria that need to be considered and agreed, we should remember what every salesperson should first know. To negotiate effectively, every salesperson should be fully familiar with:

- **Their own company's product range, capability and service levels**
- **Their prospect's product range, capability, size, key players, market position etc.**
- **The limits of all the negotiable points; how far you can go when negotiating**

What CAN we negotiate?

The items 'open to negotiation' can vary considerably. Every sale is different. In most cases, buyers are looking for the:

- Best price
- Highest quality
- Fastest delivery
- Best customer service levels

Depending on the product or service, they are also likely to want to achieve:

- The highest specification
- The greatest quality/reliability
- The widest application

In specific circumstances, they may even be looking for:

- The largest size
- The lightest colour
- The best portability

With technical or specialist products, the list of criteria or attributes may be significantly longer.

Tip: Clearly, it is essential to list all required aspects that need to be or can be negotiated. I say this because, in negotiation, it is very useful to know the difference between 'NEEDS to be negotiated' and 'COULD BE negotiated'. Meaning that if you reach a point where you cannot quite match their need, you could offer something else that is not necessarily needed but could still be valuable to the prospect.

And do not forget YOUR objectives - what YOU want to achieve.

I was once accused of putting the needs of the customer before the needs of the company that employed me. I think the phrase was 'You'd better decide who you really work for'. This was effectively a job threat if I didn't change my approach! This was from a sales director who favoured the higher-pressure approach and the same company that had the MD who told my colleague not to come back if he didn't win the order. (You may like to know that I did not change my approach; won the best deal available AND the customer came back for more!)

SET OBJECTIVES: What do YOU want to achieve?

Having the knowledge and clarity of your own objectives will help you to decide what is important. For instance, if business is good and your primary objective in targeting this prospect is to gain a strategic advantage in the market, then pricing may not be the priority in negotiation. Having clarity of objective will also help in the next step which is:

DEFINE, SET (AND STICK TO) YOUR LIMITS, i.e. know how much 'leeway' you have

As an example: if you have to negotiate on price, delivery, number and size, then starting the negotiation without knowing your limits is a recipe for disaster. You could easily end up sticking with a figure that the prospect needs to change, when prior knowledge would have told you that you have enough leeway to give them what they want and maintain the possibility of a win-win deal.

Likewise, you may decide to move things forward by dropping the price or increasing the quantity, but again, knowing your limits will tell you the price below which you will start to make a loss.

BE PREPARED WITH CONTINGENCIES

It is likely that there will come a point where an impasse is reached. Neither of you can, or are prepared to move on your position. This is where your contingency plan comes in.

Tip: Don't be too hasty with the contingency. They may be just as keen to move forward and could reduce their demands before you need to act.

Two approaches can work in this situation:

1/ Added value

- Something in reserve that could help move things along when an impasse is reached.
- Something of low cost to you, but of good value to the prospect. (The concept of Added Value is illustrated later in this chapter.)

2/ Offer to respond in a short time

- Say 24 hours, suggesting that a rethink is required to confirm priorities, check how far you can go and try and think out of the box.
- The following day, before your official response, call to check with them their level of intransigence. Considering the fact that we are having a few problems changing our offer, you can ask if they are still sticking with their position? There is a small but testable possibility that they have decided to back down, and then you do not have to.
- If nothing has changed, be ready with your alternative suggestions, your contingency.

To illustrate the power of the **'Added Value'** approach, I like to tell the story of the Florida Quays:

Selling Lobsters in Florida

Many large and expensive boats are moored regularly at the Florida Quays. Along the quays could be found many stalls, some of which sell lobsters. Apparently rich and expensive boat people enjoy rich and expensive crustaceans. When the economy slumped, most lobster sellers became involved in a price war to maintain their share of the market. As we all know, price wars lead to self-destruction, In the end, just one stall was left, and ironically, that stall had not reduced their prices!

They ADDED VALUE instead.

The had asked themselves; 'what do people like to eat with lobsters' and realised that fresh lemon juice was a favourite. Since they were in Florida where fresh lemons grow on trees, this lobster seller filled a basket with lemons and placed it in front of his stall. Above it he added a prominent sign saying 'FREE! FRESH LEMONS, HELP YOURSELF'

Human nature did the rest. The word FREE attracts. Even the idea of fresh lemons causes ones mouth to salivate. Seeing the lobsters next to the lemons caused irresistible temptation.
Many more lobsters were sold.

So, when negotiation hits a wall, have something ready to add to the offer; something that costs you little, but is of good value to them.

In the case of a product, it could be more attractive packaging, faster delivery or something that can be used with it to greater effect. With a service, it could be additional time, another associated offer that will benefit the prospect, or an add-on service that compliments in an attractive way.

So, have your lemons ready!

THE SALIENT PROCESS FOR NEGOTIATION

This has been developed, tested, tweaked and honed over many years in the field. Every sale is different, but this approach covers all bases. There are key points within the list below which allow you to retain control and lead the process while demonstrating thoroughness and clarity of purpose and reaching agreement with minimal risk to a positive result.

To summarise the essential preparation, planning, strategy and structure for negotiation:

1. **Know what the customer wants *and* needs**
2. **Identify the true decision makers and influencers**
3. **Define and prioritise your and their objectives**
4. **List the negotiation points**
5. **Decide your limits; the amount of leeway you have**
6. **Craft the offer, leaving room for negotiation**
7. **Plan the process with timings and milestones**
8. **Focus on the advantage, the USP, the benefits and the differentiators**
9. **Have added-value proposals ready, if needed; prepare your 'lemons'!**

Covering all these points will give both parties the best chance of achieving the best deal for each. Best of all it will give you the best opportunity of winning the business.

The secret of good negotiating is preparation and questioning. Preparation as outlined in the list above, and the careful application of questioning skills and techniques.

Being clear of your own intentions and limits, as well as the buyers' intentions and limits will allow you to maintain control and lead the process to be sure of securing the best deal. It is not always possible to be 100% sure of your ground, but the following should enable you to achieve the best possible results and to avoid anything unexpected or potentially distracting.

QUESTIONING

A good approach to questioning is to select, structure and pace them, in order to be sure of three essential aspects:

1. **Clarity** – both sides being clear as to what is agreed and what is/are the objective/s.
2. **Progression** – being sure that all questions and answers move the process forward to agreement.
3. **Agreement** – confirming every point to achieve gradual and then overall buy-in to the deal.

Other key questions can be used to great effect; each being used in context to achieve at least one of the three aspects above. The following examples show ways of moving forward in this way, with potential follow-on questions to achieve the needed clarity:

The first key question varies slightly depending on your target, or prospect.

- **If you are simply looking to make a sale, then the first version, and subsequent follow-on questions apply.**
- **If you are looking to build a relationship and become a valued supplier, then the second option is chosen. The difference is small but meaningful!**

a) What do we need to do to win the order?
b) What do we need to have agreed before you will be able to place the business with us?

The first option wins the prize for the 'blooming obvious', but I love its simplicity and directness. If they then outline all you need to do, and you can do it, then you can be sure of winning the order!

The second option allows for a full supplier selection process to be outlined by the buyer. Without knowledge of this process, needs and expectations will not be clear

and the potential for the lack of clarity, forward process and agreement will be significantly limited.

Subsequent questions could include:

- **'Of these negotiation points which is the most important aspect for you?** – *what is their key objective?*
- **'Is price or level of support the over-riding factor?** – *an alternative to the previous question*
- '**What is the order of importance of these negotiation points?** – *which helps you to work out where you will meet resistance to flexibility and where you may be able to offer and gain ground.*

If you are facing competition from another supplier and have hit an issue with a point of negotiation:

- **'If we offered a better product/service but were a couple of percent higher in price would you place the order with us**
- **'If we offered a slightly less comprehensive service, would you place the order with us?**

The answer to this will give a clear indication of their eagerness to buy from you, and it will give many clues as to the relative importance of different negotiation points.

Using this direct and targeted approach will provide a number of useful benefits, notably the clarity, progression and agreement we are seeking.

Other key questions that could be used when appropriate:

- **Have we reached agreement on this point?** - *Can we mark it as agreed? Putting a 'stake in the ground' helps to ensure that no attempt is made to revisit an agreed point.*
- **Does that match your need?** – *It's good to ask direct questions. If it doesn't match, ask the question(s) below.*
- **'How far are we from meeting your requirements?'** – *What more is needed to reach agreement?*
- **'Can you relax that aspect?'** – *useful when you are unable to meet one aspect of their need – and need to know how flexible they can be with that?*

Once agreement has been reached on each point then the following is essential in order to fully manage the negotiation process:

SUMMARISE, CLARIFY AND CONFIRM

Too many times during my sales career, I have experienced buyers wanting to return to a point that we have agreed already, with the aim of achieving a result more favourable to them but to the detriment of my proposal. They felt they had every right to undo all the good work we had done in reaching a mutually agreeable stage of the process.

Summarise, Clarify and Confirm, or SCC for short, is a simple 'belt-and-braces' approach that can reduce significantly the risk of any attempt to re-negotiate. It is not infallible but has worked well for me.

In simple terms:

- **At each point agreed describe it in writing,**
  or after a few points, summarise these in a list
- **Repeat and clarify each point to prevent misunderstandings**
- **Obtain full agreement to the written version, tick if necessary!**
- **Later, ideally the same day, confirm it in an email**
  (copy all decision makers and influencers)

This thorough approach helps to ensure clarity, progression and agreement, without the risk of misunderstandings or contradictions from the buyer.

CONSENSUAL NEGOTIATION

This term I use to describe the process by which you can maintain a balance of achievement and satisfaction for both parties.

GIVE SOME GROUND

At some stage, it is useful to be able to give some ground and concede an occasional point. If you find you can win every point, or you can be flexible and accommodate every need they request, then you are very likely to win the business. However, where is the job satisfaction for the buyer?

WINNING AND CONCEDING

The key here is to aim to WIN THE MAJOR POINTS and be prepared to CONCEDE MINOR POINTS. Clearly, this is only possible if you have decided which are major and minor points and how much flexibility or 'wriggle room' you have available.

I have heard of occasions when an experienced salesperson will contrive to have the buyer request some leeway for a particular point. Feigning difficulty in achieving this the seller would consider the request carefully before giving in reluctantly. Manipulative yes, and not recommended by Salient, but quite effective nonetheless. It is particularly good for improving the job satisfaction of the hard-working buyer.

Whether the point is genuine or contrived, conceding minor points helps in three ways:

- **To make the process more equal in achievement**
- **To help the buyer feel satisfaction in the process**
- **To help build a 'balanced' relationship**

Conceding minor points is a little like having lemons ready; you can add value to the process at little cost to yourself.

DEALING WITH OBJECTIONS or IMPOSSIBLE REQUESTS

At some stage in the negotiations, it is very likely that the buyer will want to interrupt the process. This will be done as:

- **An objection to a strategy, tactic or offer that you have made**
- **A sudden need to re-visit something already agreed**
- **An insistence to stick at one fact or figure, or even**
- **An unexpected delay in moving forward**

Every time this happens, it could be a genuine issue, or equally, it could be an attempt to take control of the process. The way you handle it can have a significant bearing on the outcome.

If you give in too easily, then this 'interruption' is likely to be repeated and the buyer will push for a deal that is more and more in their favour. If too intransigent, the issue could become a 'deal-breaker' from which there is no recovery.

Handling Objections is a large topic in that there are many possible types, sources and impacts to be had from objections. Likewise, there are many different approaches and strategies for dealing with such issues. For this reason, I will offer just a brief solution that should fit most situations. The full module, 'Dealing with Objections' will be part of my next book.

A simple approach to dealing with objections:

- **Always respect the request – *it may be a genuine issue***
- **Try and find its derivation – *who made the objection, and why?***
- **Try to gauge its importance – *is it a red-herring or a deal breaker?***

In order to do this, the following is a successful strategy:

1. **Respect it – *remain professional at all stages***
2. **Clarify – *ask why the change, who requested, what do they NOW need?***
3. **Protest – *if it is a need to revisit a previously agreed point, a gentle protest will ensure you keep the moral high ground, but always agree to give it a second look***
4. **Delay to consult – *this works well. Objections can be, or can become emotional exchanges. Promise to respond in 24 hours but call back after 18 hours to check if the objection/request is still valid. I have found that in many cases, without the emotion of the moment, the importance had reduced or even disappeared. Re-check the validity and importance before offering any compromise as it may no longer be needed.***

There is a fifth element to this strategy when dealing with technical businesses which is covered in my Technical Sales courses.

THE COMPETITION

Sometimes, the buyer will refer to the competition. It may be a passing comment relating to an alternative supply, or it may be a threat to buy from someone else unless you sell the exact product at the exact price...it happens!

Rule number one: never 'rubbish' the competition. Retaliation can be swift and painful.

- 'Do as you would be done by' - treat them how you would prefer they treat you – with respect and professional courtesy.

- Reminding them of the advantage and benefits you offer will help to re-focus them on why you are the best option for them.
- Avoid talking about details of competitor faults as they need to be shown how much better you are; the ***differentiators*** are key.

Differentiators are the things that **you do** which others do not do, or do not do as well, which is what makes you different.

The following are phrases you could use, depending on how 'canny' you want to be. The wording is accurate and honest; however, *the implications are clear*....

- ***'I am sure they would make a good supplier but'***
- ***'We would do more of...'***
- ***'Our offer would include...'***
- ***'We have one of the best track records in the market for...'***
- ***'I believe we offer a more personal and efficient service'***
- ***'We are proud of our reliability and professionalism'***
- ***'OUR focus is on providing exactly what the customer wants, and with more support'***

...and so on.

Emphasise the positive aspects of working with you.
Say nothing derogatory about them. It is up to you if you want to imply any shortcomings in the competition but be careful how pointed you are.

A great way of reducing the threat of the competition is to emphasise your happy customer base:
'Our customers are very loyal and keep coming back for more. I would be happy to put you in touch with one of them.'

Clearly that must be true, and it is essential to have primed your best customer to expect a call!

Another, useful technique in negotiation takes the impressive title:

THE POWER OF SILENCE

Silence, as a negotiation technique, can be very effective. Used in extreme cases, this should only be attempted by experts. Extreme?

In my early years in sales I worked with such an expert who went on to become the Sales Director. He was responsible for some of the biggest accounts within the company and so would negotiate regularly with very senior personnel. He had been working to secure a large order from a multinational aerospace manufacturer. Negotiations had taken many months and finally it had come to the moment when the order was to be placed. Our expert attended their large office and sat opposite their chief negotiator, the purchasing director. Expectations were high as our man had covered every base with his usual thoroughness and expertise. All it needed was a signature.

The contract was open at the last page and a pen was placed strategically. After pleasantries were completed, the purchasing director turned to our man and said:
'I'm sorry I cannot sign this unless you agree to a further 5% reduction.'
Our man sat there. He said nothing. He showed no expression. He waited. He continued waiting. It may only have been a few seconds but would have felt like hours.

Both sides knew exactly what was NOT being said! After a time, the director picked up the pen and, without saying a word, signed the order at full value. Conversation re-started and *nothing was said about the incident.*

This should only be attempted by the more experienced and certainly not by the faint hearted!

Much less stressful, but still to significant advantage is the technique I call:

The Short Silence, or, Respectful Pause

Again, it is not what is said, it is what is not being said that counts; it is what the silence represents that is important. Here are a couple of examples:

Someone has asked what to them is a difficult or puzzling question.
To you, it may have an easy answer. How do you respond?

The temptation is to jump in with a quick answer. The risk is that it translates as a gently mocking or condescending tone. Whatever, you say, if said immediately and quickly can sound dismissive of the question and questioner.

The same can happen in negotiation. The buyer may ask for a slight reduction here or an improvement there. You may know that this is achieved easily and are tempted to agree immediately and move on. What does this say about your original offer? Perhaps that it was over-priced or under-specified? The implication is a lack of respect for their position and willingness to 'rip-them-off'.

Eagerness to answer a good question or to reach agreement can result in a quick response or capitulation. This, in turn, shows little respect for the question or request. It can result in undermining your own credibility and diminishing their respect for you.

Pausing to think, to consider the question or request gives it the seriousness and respect it deserves. It maintains a professional approach and demeanour and helps to build further the business relationship.

THE SALIENT POINTS OF NEGOTIATION

- **Define your objectives – align them with the objective of your prospects**
- **Identify all points open to negotiation – prioritise them**
- **Confirm with the prospect their points for negotiation and their priorities**
- **For each item, know the range of options – your 'room for manoeuvre'**
- **Plan the process with timings and milestones**
- **Use techniques such as 'Adding Value', the 'Strategic Pause', 'Key Questions', 'Contingencies', dealing with the Competition, etc.**
- **Always be 'friendly with a purpose', and stick to your objectives**
- **When stuck with detail, come back to AIDA, emphasising the positives**
- **Give and take *within your pre-set limits***
- **Be firm but fair and work for a consensus**
- **At every stage, focus on the close**
- **Tick the boxes and move to agreement**

As with all parts of the sales process, preparation is key. With negotiation, sticking to your limits and accepting you have a duty to yourself and your business to achieve the best deal you can, will help ensure the best possible outcome.

Once negotiation is complete, we come to that stressful/easy*, confrontational/relationship-building* action known generally as 'CLOSING'!
(* delete to match your chosen approach)

CHAPTER 8:
CLOSING & SECURING
a.k.a. 'THE ULTIMATE CLOSE'

As stated at the beginning of the last section, negotiation and closing are best considered together. The reason for this will become clear.

I ought to remind you that 'closing' can and should be attempted throughout the sales process. Every contact should include some form of 'close'. This generally takes the form of a summary of the status reached, agreed aspects, actions; and stages.
To avoid misunderstandings, it is helpful to follow a simple structure:

1. **We have just discussed these points...**
2. **We have agreed these aspects...**
3. **The project/process/actions have reached this stage...and...**
4. **We have agreed the following actions; for you to..., and for me/us to... in the agreed timescales of...**
5. **We will meet/discuss this again on...**

In this way, expectations are well managed, and no-one can be unclear as to the way forward.

There is also the 'Interim Close' which is often a simple question such as:

- 'Are we still on course to win the business?'
- 'Is there anything else we should cover?'
- 'How far are we from completing this deal?'

Answers to these or similar questions will help maintain positive progress towards a successful outcome.

Deal Closing

Much is claimed about deal closing. In the past, this has been a very confrontational process with both sides fighting their corner and working hard to achieve the best deal, whatever it took. The actual act of closing-the-deal became a focus of opportunity for some, and a focus of dread for others. The cost of not winning the deal to the sales-person was high in business terms but could also be high on a personal level. Do you remember my story of the MD telling my colleague not to return if he didn't win the business? How stressful was *that* close?!

With the approach to negotiation which I outlined in the previous chapter, a consensual process can be undertaken, and expectations managed on both sides to a level where there should be no nasty surprises.

Integrating the following approach to closing, with the process and techniques outlined in negotiation, will provide a very simple, powerful and ethical way to *secure* the business.

The business is won because it is 'closed' suggests that there is nothing more to follow. If pressure techniques had been used in the sales process it could be unlikely that there would be a chance of more business. With ethical selling, it is far from being closed, as the prospect of future business is more certain and customer loyalty that much higher. My next book, relating to client development will show that placement of business is by no means the final action as there may well be opportunities for cross-selling, up-selling, selling more, referrals and even joint projects.

'Securing' the business is an alternative description suggesting the business is 'locked-in' with you as the supplier, and a full commitment has been made on both sides. In moving away from the confrontational approach, the act of **securing the business** has become more professional and mutually, effective and efficient. A very effective way of building a strong relationship.

Thus, engaging in ethical closing techniques will increase:

- The probability of more business from that customer, and
- The possibility of useful referrals

A question I am often asked relates to timing:
"How will I know when to close?"
You have a choice:

- Learn to be telepathic
- Become psychic
- Study degree level body language

Alternatively, you can stop worrying about timing and:

- Prepare your ground
- Fulfil their need
- Negotiate successfully and use the **'Ultimate Close'!**

I will explain......

But first, a quick check:

- ***Have all points been negotiated and agreed?***
- ***Have you Summarised, Clarified and Confirmed every point?***
- ***Have all Decision Makers and Influencers been involved and satisfied?***
- ***Is the product or service ready to be delivered?***

This last question is one that is easily overlooked. In a corporate environment, it is always a good idea to check with production or service delivery personnel, that the product or service is ready for shipment or delivery.

As an entrepreneur or small business operator, it is worthwhile checking the preparation time and free diary time to be able confirm the required delivery. It may have fit into the customer's schedule at the beginning of the process, but things may have changed. There are few things worse than achieving an order and then finding you are unable to deliver against it in the required timescales.

I once made a list of closing techniques. I counted over 50, although some were more effective than others. My favourites 'classics' are:

The Wellington Close	here you list all the positive and negative points and then convert the negative
The Elephant Close	make minor commitments to achieve greater buy-in
The 'Assumed Close'	(more for established customers) assume the deal is agreed and work backwards to a schedule
The Half-Nelson Close	(or the 'Over a Barrel' Close) if we do what you request, will you go ahead and buy from us?
The Puppy-Dog Close	let them try it out, then take it away
The Conditional Offer	NOT the 'now or never', but time limited to allow a proper decision
The Alternative Close	a choice of 2 or 3 options is more successful than a 'yes or no'
The Direct Close	please may I have the order?

In developing the **'Ultimate Close'** I have combined the best bits of some of my favourites to produce a very simple, ethical, stress-free and successful way of winning business.

'ULTIMATE' is a grand title for a very simple process. The point is, if you have prepared well and followed the full process so far, there should be no reason for there to be anything more complex than the 'Ultimate Close' which comprises:

- **a final clarification**
- **a summary and**
- **a simple question**

The process up to the point negotiation is complete could be regarding as a gentle uphill climb, whereas this part of the process becomes an even more gentle down-hill smooth slide.

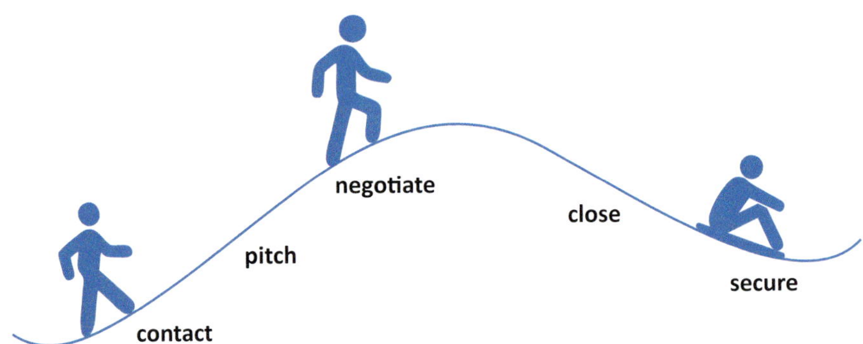

Let me show you what I mean...

The 'Ultimate Close' Process:

To close effectively we need to check the customer's decision-making process. We achieve this by starting at the desired result and working backwards (often a very effective way of project planning!)

1. **When does the product/service need to be delivered?**
   Then, taking account of our lead time – how long it takes us to deliver...
2. **When does the order need to be placed?**
   Usually, this is at the same time as the final agreement, but not necessarily
3. **When does everything need to be agreed?**
   It may take a while to raise the order if it is a larger company

4. **Who makes the decision and who needs to be involved**?
   The DM, the M.A.N. and the influencers...and finally...
5. **What needs to be agreed?**
   Make a list of all points to be negotiated and agreed, from both sides

Make this list with the prospect - and plot a timeline for the negotiation and close.
In this way, the process becomes fully involving for both sides and so achieves much greater 'buy-in' from the prospect. If they have helped to plan the process with you, they are much less likely to involve any other potential supplier.

In short, it achieves:

- **Much better involvement and buy-in from the prospect**
- **Manages expectations – both sides know exactly where they are in the process**
- **Allows better control and direction of the process**
- **Maintains momentum towards the desired result**
- **Focuses on the close, the win-win for both parties**
- **Avoids nasty surprises, effectively 'locking-in' the positive outcome**
- **Maintains the positive and mutually beneficial business relationship**

Strictly speaking, as we have now combined the negotiation and the closing process, we should call it the **'Ultimate Transaction'** instead! What's in a name?
Once we have full answers to the above questions, we then proceed to outline the full transaction process:

THE ULTIMATE TRANSACTION

The Key point is to map out the whole process with FULL CUSTOMER INVOLVEMENT AND AGREEMENT:

1. **LIST ALL THE POINTS TO NEGOTIATE AND AGREE**
   – and decide the order in which they will be addressed
2. **APPLY A TIMESCALE TO THE PROCESS**
3. **WORK THROUGH THE LIST**
   – tick and confirm every stage
4. **REVIEW AND CONFIRM AGAIN DURING THE PROCESS**
   – to secure and highlight progress
5. **REACH AND AGREE THE FINAL POINT AND THEN....**
6. **ASK FOR THE ORDER**

Asking for the order is a point where many will falter:

> ***What if they say no?***
> ***What if I've missed something?***
> ***What if I've timed it wrongly?***
> ***What if…what if…what if…***

The question everyone should ask is: ***What if I DON'T ask for the order?***

If you have done a good job, then it should be…**A FOREGONE CONCLUSION!**

If you feel that the final question is the scary bit, read on.

ASKING FOR THE ORDER

1. The confident, non-specific question (with no mention of the transaction!):
   Are you happy to go ahead with that?
2. The confident specific question (sometimes, it is better to be direct):
   Please may I have the order?
3. The cautious question (for the less confident, or if you suspect something has changed):
   Would this be a good time to ask for the order?

I love this last question. You are not actually asking for the business, but the response you receive will guide the way forward.
If they say 'yes' to this last question, then it looks like you have won the business!
If they say 'no', this is NOT necessarily a lost order/business. To turn the 'no' into a 'yes' is simple. **Find out what still needs to be done to win it; then do it and win it!**

If the full process has been done as outlined and everyone is clear about what has been achieved already and what is expected as you move forward, then I would be very surprised if they did say 'no'. However, if they do, I suggest the following way forward which can still bring success:

You are 99% of the way to success, do not accept NO!

My solution to a rejection at the last hurdle:

First, it is not necessarily a rejection. You have worked hard to reach this stage and you have earned the right to an understanding of why they said no.

1. **Apologise if appropriate, 'clearly I have missed something important'.**
2. **'Could you give me some idea as to what is missing please?**
   ...and, the key question:
3. ***What do I need to do to win the order/the business?***

What you are doing here is being a little humble and effectively handing back control to the buyer. After all, you have controlled, or at least led the process up to this point and they may wish to take over at the last moment. Unless something untoward has happened since your last contact with them, it is likely to be something small and easily sorted and achievable. Asking 'what do I need to do to win the order' is a wonderfully direct way of finding out what comes next. You have built a good working relationship. You both know you are 99% there, so the last 1% should be achievable. You are then entitled to ask the key question:

'So, if I/we do that, will you place the order with us?'

They can hardly say no, as they have just told you what to do to win it!

I love this part of the process. It becomes so simple, direct and straightforward that you can hardly fail to win, and your business conversion rates can then remain the highest possible.

ACHIEVEMENT: A happy salesperson and a happy customer!
The ULTIMATE WIN-WIN DEAL

SMEs and micro-businesses, as well as some larger businesses, may have products or services that require less to be negotiated or agreed prior to the order being placed. There may be very little to agree; perhaps just price, delivery, packaging and so on. The result may be an order achieved at the first contact. However, some of this process will still be relevant and the ultimate questions are always useful!

In every business, there comes a time when joint ventures or projects need to be considered and planned. Other parties will be involved, and this process can be valuable in these instances as well.

THE SALIENT POINTS of Negotiation and Closing (Securing)

- Linking the two creates the best chance of success
- A planned and gradually increasing 'buy-in' reduces the impact and potential stress of a final close
- It builds the relationship and makes a positive outcome significantly more likely
- Monitoring the progress with the customer helps to keep it on course
- It ensures all expectations are clear and managed well on both sides
- The 'Ultimate Question' becomes a small and easy part of the whole process
- The cautious request for the order covers all likely scenarios

CHAPTER 9:
WHAT NEXT? - MOVING FORWARD

We have covered a considerable amount of ground since page one. From the ethics of selling, through marketing for sales then on to planning and the whole sales process up to closing and securing.

The Salient approach is to follow the sales process in its simplest form and then to add in a variety of skills and techniques at every stage, with each person choosing the most appropriate for them, their business and their markets. This book has given some insight into how that works.

But that is not the whole story. Not by any means. Far from it. There is much, much more.

There is much more to be had, to be considered. There are many other ideas to be tried and adopted within the sales process and in other areas of business development. As I have stated on numerous occasions, winning the order is not the end of it. It is certainly not the 'close' as it is called. Once you have won the new customer, you should look after them, continue developing the relationship and ensure that every opportunity of achieving their business is identified and secured.

The final part of the sales process is Client Management and Development, and this is such a large subject that it deserves its own consideration, focus and book! Within it there are sections on handling objections, dealing with awkward customers, referral systems, the 'extra mile', and the essential sales management and team development. Then there are modules in time management, profile growth and campaign development, networking skills, selling yourself, high-level business relationships and so on. The psychological aspects of selling is another fascinating aspect to consider. There is so much to sales and marketing, and we have only scratched the surface. Look out for my next book which will cover these topics and more, focusing particularly on customer thinking, development and management.

In this handbook of sales, I have offered a description; an understanding of ideas, skills and techniques in ethical selling. Reading and understanding is just the first part. The real magic comes with the application of these new processes and approaches; in applying them to meet your needs, and in using them to improve your sales performance and to grow your business.

Hence the Salient training courses, the coaching sessions, the master classes, seminars and workshops! These are all geared to taking these ideas, selecting the most appropriate, and making them work for YOU in the most effective and profitable way.

Should any reader wish to discuss the possibilities of Salient helping them and their business in this way, please feel free to be in touch. Full details are available on the Salient website: www.salientsales.co.uk

You will achieve the most value from this book if you try some of these ideas, measure their affects, and then adjust, hone and perfect them for profitable use in your businesses.

I hope you have enjoyed reading this as much as I have in writing it. In the end it turned out to be very stimulating and rewarding process. I urge you to try some of the ideas we have covered. I would love to hear how you have applied them and made them work for you. Drop me an email. I will respond with pleasure.

Build good, strong customer relationships. Help them buy from you, again and again. Find some more future customers and convert them to you and your business.
Most of all:

ENJOY SELLING!